The Civil War History Series

FORT MONROE

The Key to the South

These soldiers from Company H, 3rd Massachusetts Militia were among the first reinforcements to arrive at Old Point Comfort, thereby ensuring that Fort Monroe would remain under Federal control after Virginia seceded from the Union on April 17, 1861.

On the Cover: Members of the 3rd Pennsylvania Heavy Artillery Regiment band assemble on Fort Monroe's parade field in 1864.

THE **CIVIL WAR HISTORY** SERIES

FORT MONROE

THE KEY TO THE SOUTH

JOHN V. QUARSTEIN
AND
DENNIS P. MROCZKOWSKI

Sarah Goldberger, David J. Johnson, J. Michael Moore, and Tim Smith
Photo Editors

ARCADIA
PUBLISHING

Copyright © 2000 by John V. Quarstein and Dennis P. Mroczkowski
ISBN 978-0-7385-0114-7

Published by Arcadia Publishing
Charleston SC, Chicago IL, Portsmouth NH, San Francisco CA

Printed in the United States of America

Library of Congress Catalog Card Number: 2005920754

For all general information contact Arcadia Publishing at:
Telephone 843-853-2070
Fax 843-853-0044
E-mail sales@arcadiapublishing.com
For customer service and orders:
Toll-Free 1-888-313-2665

Visit us on the Internet at www.arcadiapublishing.com

Fort Monroe's ability to dominate the entrance to Hampton Roads is clearly illustrated by this 1861 aerial perspective. The fort, supported by companion fortifications on the Rip Raps and Newport News Point, maintained the only Union position in Virginia shortly after the Civil War erupted. While the Federals controlled the north side of Hampton Roads, the Confederates countered on the south side with batteries at Sewell's Point, Craney Island, and Pig Point. Even though this stalemate would continue for a year, Fort Monroe's design and powerful armament allowed the U.S. Navy to utilize this anchorage for the North Atlantic Blockading Squadron and to blockade nearby Southern ports.

CONTENTS

FORTRESS MONROE, OLD POINT COMFORT AND HYGEIA HOTEL, V.ª
THE KEY TO THE SOUTH.

This pre-war engraving by E. Sachse and Company of Baltimore entitled "Fortress Monroe, Old Point Comfort and Hygeia Hotel, VA: The Key to the South," highlights Old Point Comfort's dual role during the antebellum era as a coastal fortification and high-society resort.

INTRODUCTION

When the British fleet sailed into Hampton Roads during the War of 1812, the Old Point Comfort Lighthouse could only welcome the invaders into the harbor. Hampton Roads and the Chesapeake Bay were virtually defenseless. Old Point Comfort lacked any type of fortification to repel the enemy fleet. Eventually the British burned Hampton and a score of other towns along the Chesapeake, including Washington, D.C. It was a national humiliation.

The lesson was not lost upon the young nation as Virginia and other coastal states clamored for an effective coastal defense system immediately following the war. Consequently, several studies were conducted by both the Army and Navy to identify the best means of coastal defense. Since the protection of Hampton Roads and the Chesapeake Bay was deemed paramount, a recommendation was made to fortify Old Point Comfort. Work commenced on the fort in earnest in 1819 and was completed by 1834.

Fort Monroe, named for President James Monroe, would become the largest moat-encircled, stone fortification in North America. Even though Fort Monroe was designed to mount 412 guns, a companion fort built on the Rip Raps was needed to effectively guard the channel. Named Fort Calhoun in honor of Secretary of War John C. Calhoun, the fort was still not finished by 1860.

Fort Monroe quickly became one of the most important military installations in the South. Brigadier General Abraham Eustis established the Artillery School of Practice at the fort in 1824. However, the fort's location overlooking Hampton Roads made Fort Monroe a perfect assembly, training, and embarkation site for troops mustered to serve in the Seminole War, Nat

Turner's Rebellion, the Black Hawk War, and the Mexican War. Accordingly, many officers destined to gain acclaim during the Civil War served at Fort Monroe during the antebellum era. Robert E. Lee supervised the construction of the fort's moat in the 1830s and his first son, George Washington Custis Lee, was born in Fort Monroe. Men like Joseph E. Johnston, Jubal Early, John A. Dix, and Robert Anderson were among the many future Civil War leaders to pass through the fort's sally ports.

The Chesapeake Bay's soothing waters and fresh sea breezes transformed Old Point Comfort into a popular resort. The Hygeia Hotel was built outside the fort's walls in 1822 and eventually expanded into one of America's grand hotels. Presidents Andrew Jackson and John Tyler used the Hygeia and a simple frame house on the Rip Raps as a summer White House. The Hygeia welcomed many other famous individuals, and its veranda was the scene of Edgar Allan Poe's last public poetry recital.

Fort Monroe, despite its luxurious setting, was designed for war. When the Civil War erupted, it would immediately become a symbol of the Union within the Confederacy. The fort's massive walls and heavy ordnance combined with the U.S. Navy's ability to resupply Fort Monroe at will made it impossible for Confederates to seize Old Point Comfort after Virginia left the Union on April 17, 1861. By May 1861, Fort Monroe was overflowing with Northern volunteers and was proclaimed the headquarters of the Union Department of Virginia with Major General Benjamin Franklin Butler as department commander. While Butler blundered his way to defeat during the Battle of Big Bethel, he would also set in motion the war's evolution into a conflict to end slavery. Butler's efforts to broaden Union control on the Peninsula resulted in his pivotal contraband of war decision in mid-May 1861. Contraband camps and schools quickly sprang up outside Fort Monroe, Camp Hamilton, and Camp Butler.

Butler also sought to employ the newest technology to enhance Union operations around Fort Monroe. Advanced weaponry, such as the rifled Sawyer gun, 12-inch rifled "Union" gun, and the massive 15-inch smoothbore Rodman gun, was mounted to challenge Confederate defenses on the south side of Hampton Roads. Balloons piloted by Jack LaMountain were utilized to observe nearby Confederate positions in the summer of 1861.

The expansion of Union power on the lower Peninsula prompted Confederates to burn the town of Hampton on August 7, 1861, to deny its use by the Federals. Ben Butler was shocked by this "wanton act of cruelty" and requested to be reassigned. He was replaced as department commander by Major General John Ellis Wool.

Wool would apply his considerable military experience to strengthen Fort Monroe's defenses. His actions enabled the Federals to use the excellent anchorage of Hampton Roads as a base for the North Atlantic Blockading Squadron. The war's first amphibious operation, Butler's expedition against Hatteras Inlet, was launched from the waters off Fort Monroe. Several other major expeditions were organized against Southern harbors during the next six months. DuPont's Port Royal operation, Burnside's Roanoke Island campaign, and Farragut's New Orleans expedition were all launched from Hampton Roads.

Fort Monroe's ability to serve as a springboard for attack prompted Major General George Brinton McClellan to select the fort as his base for the Army of the Potomac's march up the Peninsula against Richmond. McClellan's campaign, however, was immediately placed in jeopardy by the ironclad ram C.S.S. Virginia's strike against the Union fleet off Newport News Point on March 8, 1862. The destruction of two Union wooden ships was witnessed by observers lining Fort Monroe's bastions seeking to gain a glimpse of the action. Only the timely arrival of the U.S.S. Monitor stopped the Virginia's rampage. McClellan was able to proceed with his campaign because of the security provided by the Union ironclad and Fort Monroe.

McClellan's progress, however, was further hampered by Confederate Peninsula defenses, which stopped the Union Army along the Warwick River. Lincoln became so disenchanted with McClellan that he steamed to Fort Monroe aboard the revenue cutter Miami on May 6, 1862. Since the Confederate Army was already in retreat toward Richmond, Lincoln met with General Wool and Flag Officer Louis M. Goldsborough to plan an assault against Norfolk.

Lincoln believed that Norfolk's capture would result in the *Virginia*'s destruction, thereby opening the James River to Union use. On May 8, Lincoln, from the ramparts of Fort Wool on the Rip Raps, observed the U.S. Navy's failure to reduce the Confederate Sewell's Point batteries. A Federal squadron, led by the U.S.S. *Monitor*, was chased away from its objective by the C.S.S. *Virginia*. Lincoln, frustrated by this turn of events, ordered Wool to land troops at Ocean View on May 9, 1862. This action forced the Confederate evacuation of Norfolk on May 10, and the *Virginia*, left without a base, was destroyed by her crew on the following morning.

Following the Peninsula Campaign, Fort Monroe continued to serve as an important base for Union operations in Virginia. The 1863 Siege of Suffolk, Ben Butler's failed Bermuda Hundred Campaign, two amphibious operations against Fort Fisher, and Weitzel's Texas expedition were all launched from Fort Monroe. The fort's significant role in organizing these campaigns helped to seal the Confederacy's fate.

Fort Monroe was also the scene of one final effort to mediate peace between the North and South. The Hampton Roads Peace Conference, held aboard the steamer *River Queen* while anchored off Old Point Comfort on February 3, 1865, proved to be a dismal failure. The war was virtually over anyway and would end two months later. Fort Monroe's service to the nation did not end at the conflict's conclusion. The fort was destined to become the most famous prison in America. Upon his capture in Georgia, former Confederate President Jefferson Davis was imprisoned at Fort Monroe beginning on May 22, 1865. Davis, charged with treason and implicated in Lincoln's assassination, was shackled and held under the strictest guard in Casemate No. 2. Thanks to the intercessions of post surgeon Lieutenant Colonel John J. Craven, Davis's confinement was eased due to health reasons and he was eventually moved to quarters in Carroll Hall. Davis was never brought to trial and was released on May 13, 1867.

Even though Jefferson Davis's release ended Fort Monroe's Civil War service, the fort would forevermore be known as "Freedom's Fortress," for its role in achieving victory for the Union. Events on Old Point Comfort during the early stages of the conflict helped to define the war's purpose and outcome. Whether serving as a base for major operations or as a safe haven for slaves seeking freedom, Fort Monroe aptly deserved its title as the "Key to the South" during the Civil War.

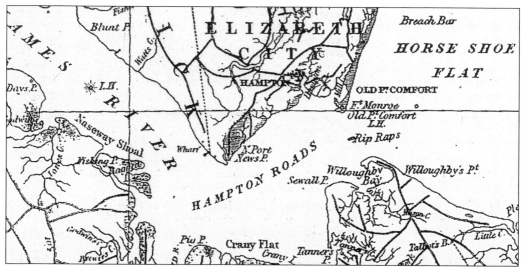

This section of Herman Boyle's 1825 map provides another view of Fort Monroe's strategic location on Old Point Comfort, which enabled the fort to defend both Hampton Roads and the lower Chesapeake Bay. Hampton Roads, formed by the confluence of the James, Elizabeth, and Nansemond Rivers, would eventually serve the Union well as a springboard for amphibious operations against Confederate harbors along the Atlantic coast.

One

GIBRALTAR
OF THE CHESAPEAKE

When the English colonists
entered Virginia waters
in 1607, one of their
first landfalls en route to
establishing a colony at
Jamestown was Old Point
Comfort. (Actually, this
small peninsula would
be called Point Comfort;
"Old" was not added to its
name until the early 18th
century.) Captain John
Smith (pictured here) called
this land spit an "Isle fit for
a Castle" in recognition of
its strategic location. The
colonists, fearful of raids
by the Spanish or the local
Powhatan Confederation,
built the first fort on Old
Point Comfort in 1609,
known as Algernourne Fort.

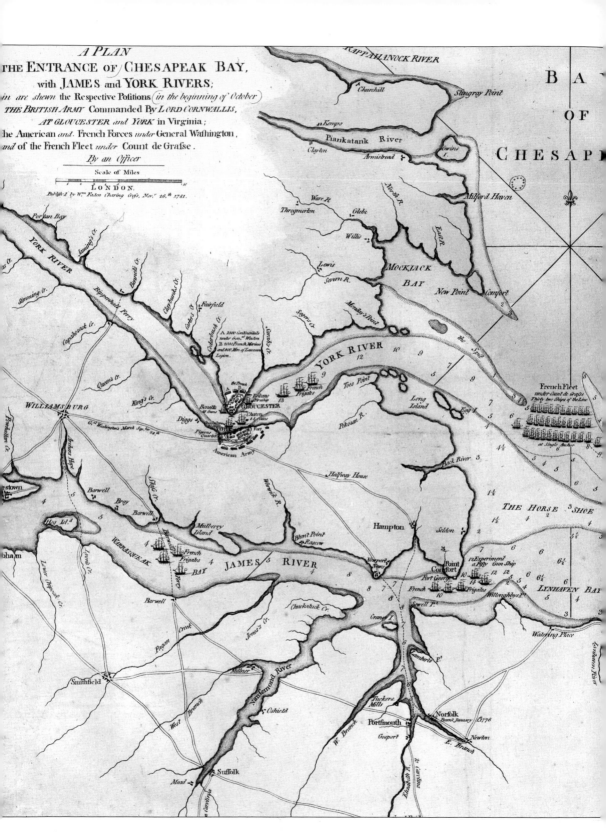

A PLAN
THE ENTRANCE OF CHESAPEAK BAY,
with JAMES and YORK RIVERS;
in are shewn the Respective Positions (in the beginning of October
THE BRITISH ARMY Commanded By LORD CORNWALLIS,
AT GLOUCESTER and YORK in Virginia;
he American and French Forces under General Washington,
and of the French Fleet under Count de Grasse.

By an Officer

Scale of Miles

LONDON.
Publish'd by W.m Faden Charing Cross, Nov.r 26.th 1781.

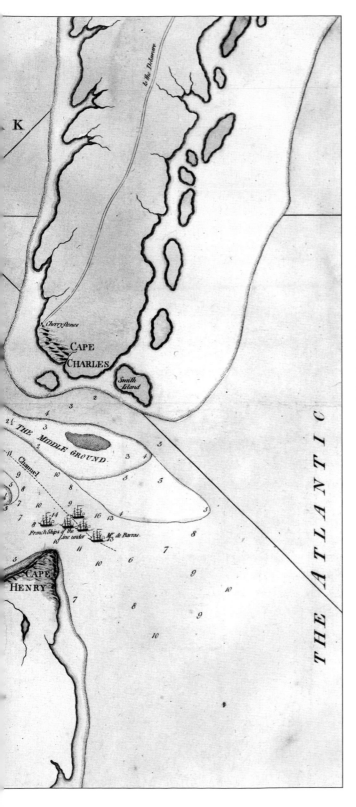

Fort Algernourne burned in 1612. Although it was quickly rebuilt, the fort eventually fell into disrepair. A more extensive fortification was constructed in 1632; however, by the time of the Second Anglo-Dutch Naval War, the fort was considered "useless." Another fort was built following a devastating 1667 Dutch raid into Hampton Roads. This fort was destroyed by a hurricane, and the harbor remained defenseless, enabling the Dutch to raid Hampton Roads again in 1673 during the Third Anglo-Dutch Naval War. Even though Old Point Comfort was reported to mount a battery containing 70 guns in 1711, a more permanent fortification was still needed. Fort George was begun in 1728 and was considered so strong that "no ship could pass it without running great risk." Unfortunately, the fort was destroyed by a hurricane in 1749 and never rebuilt. Old Point Comfort lacked fortifications during the Revolutionary War. Lord Cornwallis, commander of British forces in the Southern colonies, surveyed the site in 1781. Though only 20 miles from the Chesapeake Capes and apparently well positioned to guard the entrance to Hampton Roads, Cornwallis considered Old Point Comfort "poorly situated for defense." Thus, he moved his army to Yorktown, where it was soon trapped by a combined American-French army and forced to surrender. The French, as indicated by this 1781 map, briefly occupied Old Point Comfort during the Yorktown siege. When the French abandoned the point, it was left vacant.

11

When the Napoleonic Wars erupted in Europe, Congress was pressured to appropriate funds to create a coastal defense system. After many delays, a recommendation was made and money appropriated to fortify Old Point Comfort. Before any work could begin, however, Thomas Jefferson assumed office as president. Jefferson, believing that coastal defenses were too costly, canceled the appropriation. Consequently, when the United States declared war on Great Britain in 1812, only the recently erected lighthouse (1802) stood on Old Point Comfort.

Control of the Chesapeake Bay was one of Britain's primary strategic aims during the War of 1812. In June 1813, Admirals Sir John Borlase Warren and Sir George Cockburn sailed into Hampton Roads and positioned their fleet off Newport News Point. The British attempted to capture Norfolk on June 22, but were repulsed by hastily erected fortifications on Craney Island. Cockburn was enraged by this defeat and sacked the town of Hampton on June 25, 1813. The British continued their rampage throughout the Chesapeake Bay, eventually burning Washington, D.C., in August 1814, as depicted in this engraving.

The War of 1812 clearly indicated the need for a more effective defensive system to protect the nation's harbors and cities from naval attack. Consequently, Congress authorized a board of officers to recommend the fortifications necessary for an adequate coastal defense. Brigadier General Simon Bernard, a distinguished French military engineer and former aide-de-camp to Napoleon, was selected by President James Madison to head the board. The Bernard Board, in conjunction with an 1817 U.S. Navy report, called for the establishment of a major naval depot in the James River, and recommended that Old Point Comfort be immediately fortified. Eventually the Bernard Board would develop a comprehensive system of defense for Hampton Roads capable of withstanding a concerted siege. This system featured an enclosed work on Old Point Comfort and a castellated fort on the Rip Rap Shoal connected by a boom raft. The two forts offered "mutual protection, and to embrace in the total, the power to resist any force which may be brought against the pass into Hampton Roads." General Bernard personally designed both fortifications and his aide, Captain William T. Poussin, completed the drawings.

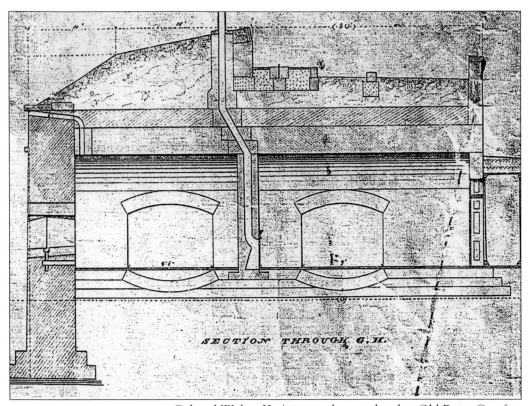

SECTION THROUGH G.H.

Colonel Walter K. Armistead was ordered to Old Point Comfort on April 21, 1817, to begin organizing materials for the fort's construction. Initially, stone from the York River was selected; however, stone acquired from Potomac River quarries was used. A wharf, "sufficiently large and substantial to allow three vessels to come alongside and unload at the same time," was constructed beginning on August 1, 1818, under the supervision of Lieutenant James Maurice. Major Charles Gratiot (pictured at left) was assigned as the superintendent of the fort's construction and work commenced in March 1819.

Fort Monroe, named for President James Monroe, would become the largest moat-encircled, masonry fortification in the United States. The fort covered 63 acres, with the circumference of its walls over a mile in length. The 8-foot-deep moat, fed by sluice gates drawing water from Mill Creek, varied in width from 60 feet at the East Gate to 150 feet at the Main Sally Port. The fort's irregular plan featured seven fronts with large bastions. The bastions protected the fort from attack at any angle with direct, flank, or crossfire. The primary concentration of fire was in the First, Second, Third, and Fourth Fronts facing the water approaches to Hampton Roads. The First, Second, and Third Fronts were casemated with a barbette tier of cannon to maximize firepower toward the harbor and channel. The Fourth Front only had a barbette tier of guns facing seaward toward the Chesapeake Bay. A water battery, designed to mount 40 casemated guns, was constructed forward of the Fourth Front as part of the outworks to increase the fort's firepower against vessels that might attack the harbor or the fort itself.

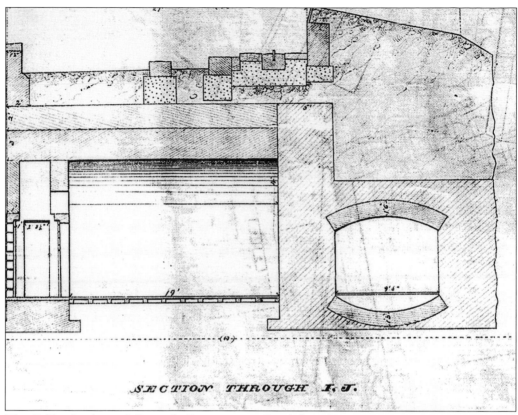

SECTION THROUGH I. J.

The Fifth, Sixth, and Seventh Fronts were all solid with a barbette tier of guns. The Fifth Front faced the landed approaches to the fort. The Fifth and Sixth Fronts were further protected by outworks, including a redan and redoubt. Fort Monroe was originally designed to mount 380 guns, but this was increased to 412. The armament ranged from small 24-pound howitzers mounted in the bastions for flank protection to the 42-pounders mounted in the Water Battery. Fort Monroe was intended to house a wartime garrison of 2,625 officers and men.

Work continued on the fort at a rapid pace. The Army used slaves, contractors, and after 1820, military convict laborers. The fort was considered three-quarters complete by spring 1822 and was beginning to look formidable. An 1823 report from the chief of engineers noted the ". . . exterior wall, ten feet thick at its base, is carried on an average all around the place to a height of twelve feet, and a wet ditch surrounds the whole work. A battery on the covert-way is constructed, capable of receiving forty-two pieces, and in the three fronts of the fortress on the sea side embrasures are partly constructed for eighty-four guns; so that, in case of necessity, a battery of one hundred and twenty-six heavy guns might be readily mounted for the protection of Hampton Roads." Captain Andrew Talcott (pictured at right) was one of several engineer officers who supervised the construction of Fort Monroe between 1819 and 1834.

The first active duty troops, Captain Mann P. Lomax's Co. G, 3rd U.S. Artillery, arrived at Fort Monroe on July 25, 1823, to act as guards for the convict laborers. In spring 1824, another 10 artillery companies were assigned to the fort to form the "Artillery Corps for Instruction." Brevet Brigadier General John Rogers Fenwick was selected by Secretary of War John C. Calhoun to command the school. Since Fenwick would only serve on Fort Monroe for a few months, the task of organizing the Artillery School of Practice fell upon the able shoulders of Brevet Colonel Abraham Eustis of the 4th U.S. Artillery. Eustis (pictured here) organized a two-year course of instruction for officers and men. The curriculum included gunnery practice, infantry drill, and laboratory instruction. A nearby 800-acre farm, the "Buck Roe Farm," was leased to provide space for gunnery and field duty training. Major General Jacob Brown noted that the school enhanced "habits of uniformity and accuracy in practical routines of service, fresh incitement to the cultivation of military knowledge, emulation, and esprit de corps among the troops, and mutual conformity and general elevation of individual character among the officers." Eustis was reassigned in 1828; however, his Artillery School of Practice set a high standard for U.S. Army schools.

One of the more distinguished individuals to supervise Fort Monroe's construction was Second Lieutenant Robert E. Lee. Lee was assigned as an assistant to Captain Andrew Talcott. Talcott, however, was absent during much of Lee's tour at Fort Monroe, which enabled Lee to gain a great deal of fortification building and construction management experience. During his tour of duty on Old Point Comfort, Lee supervised construction of the fort's counter scarp wall, designed several buildings and wharves, managed accounts and laborers, and coordinated work on Fort Calhoun's foundation. Lee and his wife, Mary Custis Lee, lived in Quarters No. 17 (The Tuileries) and their first child, George Washington Custis Lee, was born in Fort Monroe in 1831.

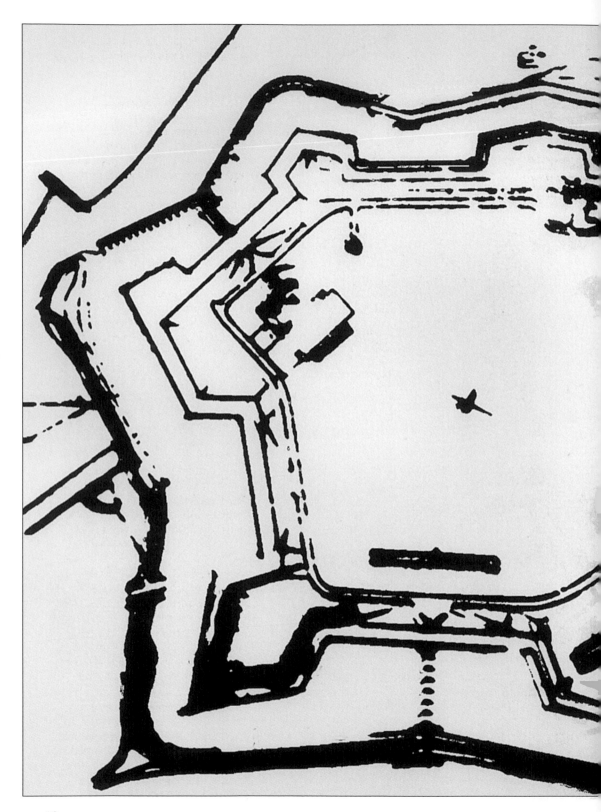

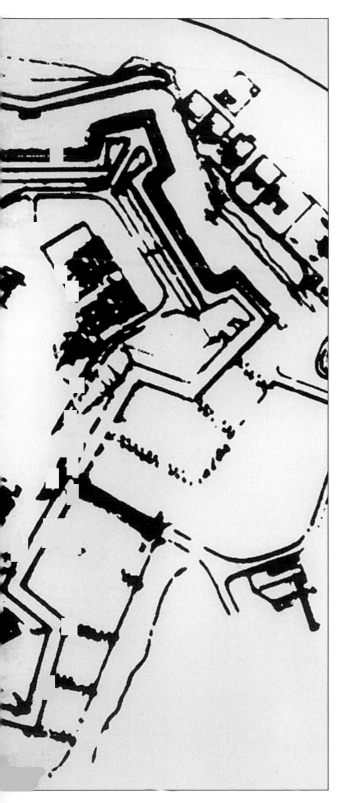

The U.S. Army Chief of Engineers reported in 1834 that "all permanent parts of this work were completed last year." The fort's cost, tabulated in 1834, totaled $1,889,840. This expense was considered too costly by some members of the U.S. Army establishment, who disliked the Frenchman General Bernard's involvement in the coastal defense project. Colonel Joseph G. Totten noted that Fort Monroe's design was based on the exaggerated scale of warfare to which Europe was then accustomed. Fort Monroe, as indicated by this 1832 plan drawn by Robert E. Lee, was indeed a huge work and the largest in the Third Coastal Defense System. Totten thought that "Fort Monroe might have been as strong as it is now against a water attack, or an assault, or a siege, with one-third its present capacity, and perhaps at no more than half its cost. We do not think this work too strong for its position, nor too heavily armed; and as the force of the garrison will depend mainly on the extent of the armament, the error has caused an excess in the first outlay chiefly, but will not involve much useless expense after completion." Because of Fort Monroe's role defending Hampton Roads, the lower Chesapeake Bay, and the U.S. Navy's major base at Gosport Navy Yard, the U.S. Army continued to improve the fort's defensive capabilities. In an 1845 report, the chief of engineers stated that the "work yet to be done, in order to give this fort its entire efficiency, comprises the following objects: the construction of the stone revetment of the counter scarp; completing furnaces and bridges; building a detached magazine; modifying the principal magazine; paving the ditch . . . embarking and grading portions of the glacis, finishing the redoubt and the caponniere leading thereto; constructing the batter deau, and painting various walls of the fort."

Old Point.

Brevet Brigadier General John E. Wool inspected Fort Monroe's armament in 1835 and noted that only 35 heavy guns were mounted in battery. In 1836, the War Department estimated that the completion of Fort Monroe's armament would require a tremendous amount of ordnance. The casemates needed sixteen 24-pounders, thirty-two 32-pounders, and ninety 42-pounders. Armament plans specified thirty 24-pounders, fifty 32-pounders, and fifty 42-pounders for mounting as barbette guns. The fort also required fifteen 10-inch heavy mortars, eight 10-inch light mortars, and ten howitzers. The estimated cost for these 301 guns was $500,000 and was over 100 guns less than was called for in Bernard's design. Even though the fort never reached its expected gun capacity, by 1834 Fort Monroe's arsenal became the fifth largest in the United States, employing 39 workmen. The arsenal's expansion was an outgrowth of the Artillery School's laboratory instruction. Officers were taught the care and manufacture of powders. The arsenal specialized in seacoast ordnance and manufacturing seacoast gun carriages. In 1841, it was one of four manufacturing arsenals in the United States.

Since Fort Monroe had several missions to perform, many officers who would gain acclaim during the Civil War served or passed through the fort from the 1820s until 1860. A young Joseph E. Johnston was assigned to Fort Monroe as a second lieutenant of artillery during Nat Turner's Rebellion. John A. Dix, who later served as President James Buchanan's secretary of the treasury and as a major general of volunteers during the Civil War, was stationed at the fort during the 1820s as an artillery captain. U.S. Army Inspector General John E. Wool reviewed the garrison and inspected the fort in 1825. Jubal Early and James Kemper, both Virginia politicians and both destined to become Confederate generals, mustered their troops at Old Point Comfort during the Mexican War. Other future Confederate generals to pass through Old Point Comfort include Walter Gwynn and Samuel Cooper. Several other future Union generals also served at Fort Monroe, such as the "hero of Fort Sumter," Robert Anderson (pictured here); Daniel Tyler; William Morris; and James W. Ripley, who became chief of ordnance during the Civil War.

Not everyone traveled to Fort Monroe by their own free will. The first "political" prisoner held at the fort was Chief Black Hawk following his defeat during the 1832 Black Hawk War. Black Hawk and several of his followers were sent to Washington, D.C. to meet with President Andrew Jackson. In turn, Jackson sent them to Fort Monroe in late April 1833 to be detained. Black Hawk only spent a few weeks at Fort Monroe. The chief was "restricted only to the garrison" and formed a friendship with post commander Abraham Eustis. Black Hawk and his followers, Whirling Thunder and the Prophet, became "the objects of much curiosity" and were constantly "beset by visitors who crowded to see them from all quarters" until they left Fort Monroe on June 4, 1833.

HYGEIA HOTEL.

When the construction of Fort Monroe began in 1819, there was a critical need to provide accommodations for engineers, contractors, and construction workers. Therefore, the U.S. Army granted permission to a group of investors led by Marshall Parks to build a hotel on Old Point Comfort. Named for the Greek goddess of health, the Hygeia was constructed in 1822 south of the main gate across from that portion of the moat that faces west. The Hygeia continued to expand over the years and in 1841 was called "large and commodious." Old Point Comfort, with steamboat connections to Norfolk, Richmond, Washington, and Baltimore, quickly became the most fashionable resort in the South. Visitors enjoyed the waters and sea breezes as well as entertainments provided by the fort's band and evening parades. An added attraction was the naval rendezvous of foreign warships in Hampton Roads during the hurricane season. Special receptions, balls, and other gala affairs aboard ships or on the Hygeia's veranda made Old Point Comfort the choice resort for the Southern elite.

Old Point Comfort also became a resort for two presidents. President Andrew Jackson first visited Fort Monroe on July 9, 1829. The next day Jackson, accompanied by several politicians and generals including Secretary of War John H. Eaton and Brigadier General Simon Bernard, toured the Hampton Roads region. On his return from Norfolk, the President visited the Rip Raps to review progress on Fort Calhoun. Jackson was impressed with the little island and returned to the Rip Raps for ten days of rest during the Peggy Eaton Controversy in August. Jackson returned again in 1831, 1833, and 1834. "His hotel at the Rip-Raps is a delightful summer residence," one newspaper noted, "freely inviting the breeze over the waters from every point of the compass, and with the polite and attentive host of the Hygeia, Mr. Marshall Parks, to cater for his table, he cannot be otherwise than 'comfortable.' " Peninsula native John Tyler was the other president to summer on Old Point Comfort and the Rip Raps. When Tyler's first wife, Letita Christian Tyler, died, the President sought the seclusion of the Rip Raps. Tyler returned again in 1844 when he married Julia Gardiner and spent their month-long honeymoon at Old Point Comfort. The couple returned to the Hygeia one year later to celebrate their first anniversary. President Millard Fillmore also visited Fort Monroe on June 21, 1851.

Another illustrious visitor to Old Point Comfort was Edgar Allan Poe. On December 20, 1828, Private E.A. Perry reported to duty on Fort Monroe. Perry was Poe's alias, which he used upon enlisting following his dismissal from the University of Virginia. Poe was promoted to sergeant major on January 1, 1829, and soon revealed his true identity and literary skills to his commanding officer, Lieutenant Joshua Howard. Poe, with Howard's assistance, was eventually able to secure his discharge by hiring a substitute. Poe then left Fort Monroe on April 22, 1829, and entered the United States Military Academy, where he served until his dismissal on March 6, 1831. Poe returned to Old Point Comfort two weeks before his death. He gave his last public poetry recital on the Hygeia's veranda, and then left for Baltimore, where he died on October 7, 1849.

One military weakness of Old Point Comfort, which was recognized by Lord Cornwallis in 1781, was that its guns could not totally command the main shipping channel leading into Hampton Roads. Complete control of the channel could only be achieved by building a companion work to Fort Monroe on the Rip Raps. The Rip Raps consisted of a shoal located almost a mile from Old Point Comfort in the middle of the entrance to Hampton Roads. This required engineers to first create an artificial island of stone upon which a tower battery, named Fort (or Castle) Calhoun in honor of then Secretary of War John C. Calhoun, was to be built. The project encountered serious foundation problems. It was not until 1860, under the able direction of Colonel Rene DeRussy (pictured here), that Castle Calhoun neared completion.

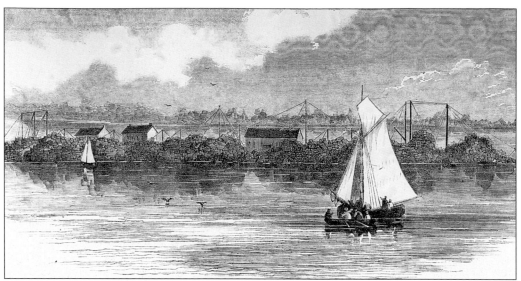

Brigadier General Simon Bernard planned Fort Calhoun as a tower battery with three tiers of casemates and an interior crest measuring 381 yards. The fort was designed to mount 232 guns and house a wartime garrison of 1,130 officers and men. Foundation work on the artificial island began in 1823 and was completed in 1825. After a year to allow the stone to settle, construction of the actual fort began in 1826. An elaborate ceremony was held on September 17, 1826, "to lay the first corner stone of this great national work of defense." Major General Jacob Brown, commanding general of the U.S. Army, was present and placed the cornerstone. Work immediately began in earnest on the fort; however, once the walls and piers had been built to the second tier level, it was discovered that the added weight caused the foundation to sink. The project was suspended and more stone was used to strengthen the foundation. The fort had sunk 6 inches by 1831. The U.S. Army already had invested $1,380,333.68 on Fort Calhoun and the total cost was estimated at $2,014,816.48.

Colonel Rene DeRussy resumed work on Fort Calhoun in 1858, yet the fort differed from its original plan. DeRussy finished 52 casemates of the lower tier and fitted them with iron-throated embrasures designed by James Totten. These casemates were ready for guns. The scarp walls and piers on the second tier facing the channel were constructed nearly to the height of the embrasure lintels. Work on the second tier included fitting the embrasure iron and paving the casemate floors. By 1860 preparations were underway for mounting guns, but the fort was far from complete.

A terrible explosion erupted in the mixing room of the Fort Monroe Arsenal's laboratory on June 22, 1855. The explosion, caused by mixing pyrotechnics, completely destroyed the arsenal and seriously damaged an adjoining building. Three men were in the arsenal's mixing room when the explosion occurred. One man, Artificer Francis M. Knight, was killed outright and another, Artificer Henry Sheffis, died three days later. Only Lieutenant Julian McAllister, although badly burned, survived. McAllister (pictured here with his wife) believed his life was preserved only due to divine intervention, and he sought to construct a chapel in recognition of God's mercy.

The Chapel of the Centurion (pictured here) was built under the direction of Post Commander Brevet Colonel Harvey Brown. Captain Alexander B. Dyer was the agent and superintendent of construction. McAllister was the principal donor. The chapel, designated for Protestant worship and open to all denominations, was consecrated on May 3, 1858, by Assistant Bishop John Johns of the Diocese of the Protestant Episcopal Church of Virginia. Two years later, another church was constructed on Old Point Comfort. This house of worship was a Roman Catholic chapel and called St. Mary Star of the Sea.

Since the beginning of its construction in 1819, Fort Monroe had grown into one of the nation's most important U.S. Army installations. Besides its coastal defense, arsenal, and Artillery School missions, it developed into a major base for operations throughout the South. The fort was first called upon for defensive action during the August 1831 Nat Turner's Rebellion in nearby Southampton County. Fort Monroe immediately sent three companies to thwart the rebellion, but the local militia had already put down the revolt before they arrived and the soldiers returned to the fort in six days. Fear of other slave revolts in New Bern and Beaufort, North Carolina, prompted the dispatch of troops in 1831 and 1833. Social unrest also resulted in the transfer of troops from Fort Monroe to disaffected regions. During the Nullification Crisis of 1832, several artillery companies were ordered to Fort Moultrie in Charleston Harbor to be on guard to enforce Federal law. As this crisis dissipated, problems arose associated with the cession of lands to the Creek Indians in Alabama, which required troops from Fort Monroe.

When war with the Seminole Indians erupted in 1835, several artillery companies were ordered from Fort Monroe to Florida. Manpower needs were so great during the war that in January 1839, the garrison could only muster three officers and nine enlisted men present for duty. Nevertheless, in 1837, the nation was divided into military departments, and Fort Monroe, with Brevet Brigadier General Abraham Eustis commanding, became headquarters of Department No. 4 (South Carolina, North Carolina, and Virginia). Troops, however, were sent out of the district in 1838 to Sacket's Harbor, New York, and Swanton, Vermont, during the Mackenzie Rebellion in Canada. Departmental reorganizations in 1842 and 1848 resulted in Fort Monroe, with Brevet Brigadier General James Bankhead commanding, remaining as headquarters of an expanded Department No. 4. Fort Monroe was made a muster center for recruits and volunteer regiments from Virginia and North Carolina during the Mexican War. These units and several artillery companies embarked from Hampton Roads to New Orleans.

Fort Monroe appeared well seasoned, after almost 30 years of service, to serve the nation as the crisis between North and South gravitated toward war. Yet Fort Monroe was virtually devoid of troops as secession split the nation. The major question in the spring of 1861 was not about the military capabilities of Fort Monroe, but whether it would be controlled by the Union or the new Confederacy during the approaching conflict.

Two

THE KEY TO THE SOUTH

When Abraham Lincoln's election set in motion the secession of several Southern states, Fort Monroe immediately became a place of extreme strategic significance for the government striving to hold together the fragmented nation. Fort Monroe had already played a role in events leading to the secession crisis when its commanding officer, Brevet Colonel Harvey Brown, dispatched troops to Harper's Ferry to help quell John Brown's raid. John Brown was already a prisoner by the time the troops reached Harper's Ferry, and they returned to the fort. Company A, 1st U.S. Artillery was then sent from Fort Monroe on November 20, 1859, for guard duty during the execution of Brown and his followers. The impending crisis prompted post engineer Colonel Rene DeRussy to complete various repairs and improvements to the fort during 1860. Despite DeRussy's efforts to repair magazines, gun platforms, drawbridges, and other defensive features, the fort was not completely armed. Furthermore, its garrison did not meet wartime standards following the bombardment of Fort Sumter in Charleston Harbor.

Lieutenant Colonel Justin Dimick was placed in command on November 30, 1859. Dimick, an 1819 graduate of the U.S. Military Academy and well trusted by U.S. Army Commanding General Winfield Scott, strove to prepare Fort Monroe for war. In early January 1861, he placed 31 additional barbette guns. The fort's garrison, however, was reduced on several occasions during the secession crisis to maintain forts in the lower South under government control. Dimick sent four companies aboard the USS *Brooklyn* in an effort to reinforce Fort Sumter on December 31, 1860. The troops left with orders to "Manage everything as secretly and confidently as possible." The mission failed, however, on January 23, 1861. Company A, 1st U.S. Artillery was detached to reinforce Fort Pickens in Pensacola, Florida. These reductions seriously depleted the already small garrison.

When Virginia seceded from the Union following the fall of Fort Sumter, the Virginia militia immediately sought to gain possession of Federal installations they claimed were the rightful property of the Sovereign State of Virginia. The Virginia militia had two targets before them in Hampton Roads: Fort Monroe and Gosport Navy Yard. Since Fort Monroe appeared sufficiently strong to repel any attack that Virginia troops could muster, they focused their efforts on Gosport. The yard was quickly surrounded and ordered to surrender. Union Secretary of the Navy Gideon Welles recognized the need to save the yard and the ships berthed at Gosport. Unfortunately, the yard commandant Flag Officer Charles Stewart McCauley vacillated and did not act to preserve the yard and its resources for the Union. Captain Horatio Wright was ordered to proceed to the yard with Flag Officer Hiram Paulding's task force and defend Gosport. Wright secured elements of the 3rd Massachusetts from Fort Monroe and steamed up the Elizabeth River on the early evening of April 20, 1861. When they arrived, the yard and ships were already being destroyed. Wright's task force returned to Fort Monroe the next morning after assisting with demolition duties.

Once Gosport fell under Confederate control, Fort Monroe became the only pre-war Federal military installation retained by the Union in Virginia. Winfield Scott increased the flow of troops to reinforce the fort. Dimick reported that the 3rd Massachusetts, commanded by Colonel David W. Waldrop, and the 4th Massachusetts, commanded by Colonel Abner B. Packard (pictured here), were on duty at Fort Monroe. He further advised Scott that over 200,000 rations and "a sufficient amount of ammunition for immediate use" had arrived. The roll call on April 28, 1861, indicated that Dimick had 62 officers and 1,134 men stationed at the fort.

Winfield Scott continued to send more troops, armaments, and supplies to Fort Monroe. When Scott advised Dimick on April 30, 1861, that fourteen 10-inch Columbiad barbette carriages, twenty-eight 42-pounder barbette carriages, and twelve 8-inch Columbiad barbette carriages were en route to the fort, he noted that "Fort Monroe is by far the most secure post now in the possession of the U.S., against any attack that can be possibly made upon it, independent of the war vessels, the *Cumberland* and the *Niagara*, at hand, and approaching you."

On May 13, Fort Monroe welcomed the 778 rank and file of the 1st Vermont, commanded by Colonel J. Wolcott Phelps, and two additional companies, totaling 132 officers and men of the 3rd Massachusetts. This brought Fort Monroe's troop strength to 2,154 men. Consequently, Dimick needed to secure a better water supply for the influx of soldiers arriving at the fort. On May 13, Dimick informed Colonel Charles K. Mallory, commander of the local 115th Virginia Militia Regiment, that he intended to take possession of a well on the Elizabeth City County side of Mill Creek. That same day Dimick took elements of the 4th Massachusetts (of which the Hancock Light Guard is shown in this photograph) and occupied both the Mill Creek Bridge and the Clark Farm. Local volunteers serving as pickets were outraged by the Union advance and swore "vengeance on Massachusetts troops for the Invasion of Virginia." One cavalry vidette, Dr. William R. Vaughan, confronted Dimick and demanded the following: "By what right, sir, does your army cross that bridge and invade the sacred soil of Virginia?" Dimick reportedly snapped, "By God, sir, might makes right!"

Mallory was shocked by the Union action and called the local militia into service. Major Benjamin Stoddert Ewell, former president of the College of William and Mary and 1832 graduate of the U.S. Military Academy, secured an interview with Colonel Dimick on May 14, 1861, to ascertain the Union commander's intentions. Dimick advised Ewell, who was then commander of the Williamsburg Junior Guard, that he only needed the well for the health of his troops. Ewell inquired if the Federals had any other plans to move against Hampton. Dimick's reply was noted by Ewell: "He laughed at the idea of violence being contemplated toward Hampton. He expressed great regret at the present state of things, and was kind and conciliatory. We agreed that it might be better for the guards not to approach too closely together. Accordingly I have orders to the guards from Hampton not to go further than within half a mile of the fort . . ." Ewell could do little to contest the Union advance, as there were only 820 men and 300 flintlock muskets available to defend the Hampton area.

Union troops, like the members of the 5th New York Infantry, continued to reinforce Fort Monroe throughout May, and soon the fort was overflowing with soldiers. Virginia volunteers were powerless to halt the flow of men and materials into the fort. As long as the Confederates lacked naval forces capable of blockading Old Point Comfort, Fort Monroe could be reinforced at will by the U.S. Navy. Furthermore, the fort's comprehensive design and armaments made it impossible for the Confederates to besiege Fort Monroe. In its first test of war, Fort Monroe's well-selected location on Old Point Comfort ensured its security and ability to serve the Union as a base of operations.

Despite Dimick's promises to Ewell, Federal soldiers continued to expand their positions on the Hampton side of Mill Creek. Massachusetts troops converted former President John Tyler's summer home, Villa Margaret, into barracks. His wife, Julia, strove to rid her home of "these scum of the earth." She asked Northern authorities to protect her property. Her protestations, however, were ignored and various Union units continued to use Villa Margaret as housing during the next few months.

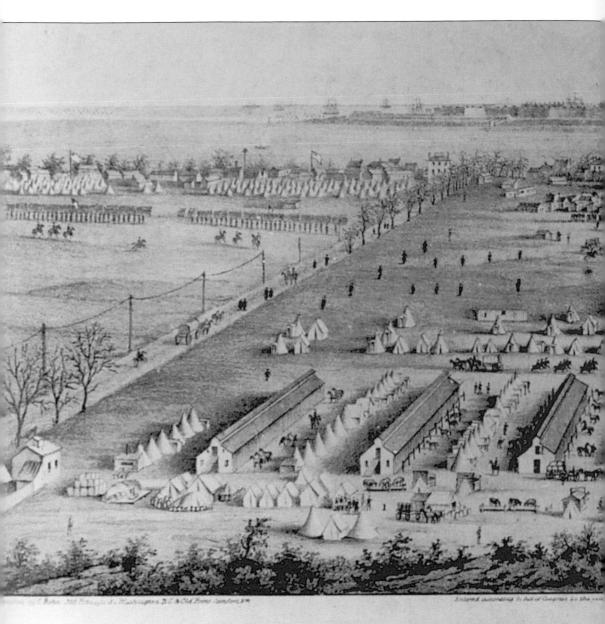

1. Grounds on Segar's Farm.

CAMP HAMILTON, FORT

Overcrowding in the fort prompted the establishment of an entrenched camp on the Segar Farm. Initially known as Camp Troy, it was soon renamed Camp Hamilton in honor of Lieutenant Colonel Schuyler Hamilton, Winfield Scott's military secretary. The 2nd New York and the 1st Vermont were billeted at Camp Hamilton upon their arrival on the Peninsula. Camp Hamilton primarily consisted of tents and other temporary structures laid out in company streets. Due to the protection provided by the guns of Fort Monroe, little effort was

SS MONROE & RIP-RAPS, V^A

made to provide the camp with extensive fortifications. The soldiers stationed at Camp Hamilton spent much of their time drilling, standing guard, attending such diversions as Bible classes, or becoming entrepreneurs. Alfred Bond made a tidy profit selling cigars to other volunteers. Bond recorded one telling reflection in his diary, writing, "In Camp Hamilton. Weather cloudy with rain at night and windy. The day is past and gone. The evening shades appear; Oh may we all remember well, The night of Death draws near."

One of the more colorful units to arrive at Fort Monroe in spring 1861 was the 5th New York. The unit, also known as Duryee's Zouaves, was formed by Colonel Abram Duryee and mustered into service on April 25, 1861. Duryee, a wealthy New York merchant and formerly in the New York state militia, modeled his unit after the colorful dress of the French Algerian light infantry. The 5th New York was noted for its unique uniform as well as its precise parade-ground drill and contained many leading New York citizens. Unit members Gouverneur K. Warren, H. Judson Kilpatrick, Joseph E. Hamblin, Henry E. Davies, and Abram Duryee all eventually became Union generals. Upon their arrival at Fort Monroe, the Zouaves encamped at Camp Hamilton.

By the end of May 1861, there were 4,451 officers and men assigned to Fort Monroe. Other than the 415 officers and men of the United States Regulars, the rest consisted of volunteer soldiers from Massachusetts, New York, and Vermont. It was a sizeable force; yet, since the volunteers were so hastily assembled and transferred to Fort Monroe, there were numerous supply problems. This scene depicts the officers of Duryee's Zouaves at Camp Hamilton as well fed. However, Colonel Joseph B. Carr of the 2nd New York reported than his men "sometimes stood sentinel with naked feet and almost naked bodies." Regardless of these problems, the large command assembled at and around Fort Monroe was destined to begin the first aggressive movement into Virginia territory.

Three

BUTLER TAKES COMMAND

The rapid increase of Union forces
on the lower Peninsula prompted
Winfield Scott to assign Major General
Benjamin Franklin Butler to assume
command of Fort Monroe on May 18,
1861. Butler, a cross-eyed lawyer and
politician from Massachusetts, had
already gained fame during the war
when he helped to end Maryland's
secessionist movement following the
April 19, 1861 Baltimore riots. Since
Butler was already commander of the
Union Department of Annapolis, he
protested this re-assignment. When
Scott indicated that the duties included
command of the newly created Union
Department of Virginia, Butler accepted.
Butler was then detailed by Scott to
work in conjunction with the U.S. Navy
and move aggressively against nearby
Confederate defenses.

"Boldness in execution is nearly always necessary," Scott advised Butler. The new commander of the Union Department of Virginia intended to immediately act upon this advice once he arrived at Fort Monroe. On May 23, Butler ordered Colonel J. Wolcott Phelps to march his 1st Vermont into Hampton to disrupt the voting on Virginia's Ordinance of Secession. John Baytop Cary and a few volunteers from his "camp of instruction" attempted to burn the Hampton Creek Bridge to block the Vermonters' advance. When Cary learned that Phelps's only purpose was to reconnoiter, Confederates and Federals joined together to extinguish the flames. Phelps then marched into Hampton, closed the polls, and then returned to Fort Monroe. Once the Federals left town, the Hamptonians immediately reopened the polls and overwhelmingly voted for secession. While Hampton residents may have been in an uproar over the Union advance, local African Americans were overjoyed. They welcomed the bluecoats with "Glad to see you." This first encounter between bondsmen and Union soldiers prompted three slaves owned by Colonel Charles K. Mallory of the 115th Virginia Militia to take "advantage of the Terror prevailing among white inhabitants . . ." and escape into the Union lines.

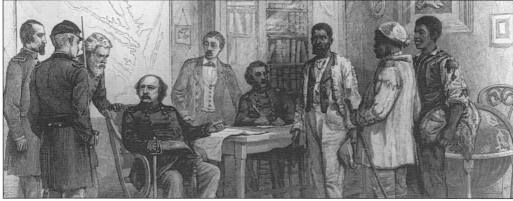

Even before the Confederates learned about these runaway slaves, Cary went to Fort Monroe to learn from Butler "how far he intended to take possession of Virginia soil." Butler advised Cary that the Federals just required more land for encampments and inferred that they would not act aggressively unless molested by Confederate troops. The next day, May 24, 1861, Cary returned once again to Fort Monroe to retrieve Mallory's slaves. Cary demanded the return of Mallory's property citing the Fugitive Slave Law as justification. Realizing that slaves were being used to build nearby Confederate fortifications, Butler refused Cary's request. He informed Cary that since Virginia now considered itself an independent nation, his "constitutional obligations" under the Fugitive Slave Law were null and void. Butler further noted that since Virginia was at war with the United States he intended to take possession of whatever property his troops required. Since slaves were considered "chattel property," Butler called Mallory's runaways "contraband of war" and assigned them to support Union operations.

The "contraband of war" decision brought slavery to the forefront as a wartime issue. Even though President Abraham Lincoln initially enforced the Fugitive Slave Law, the war now grew far beyond an effort just to preserve the Union. Ben Butler immediately recognized the political and economic implications of his contraband decision. Instead of slaves supporting the Southern economy and war effort, Butler turned this Southern asset into a Union benefit as he put the contrabands to work building fortifications as well as other related duties. Butler believed that the work of contrabands was a good return for the food and shelter provided for them. The Union general's radical opinion was often called "Butler's fugitive slave law." On August 6, 1861, Congress formally approved Butler's action in an act which "confiscated any slave who had been used for a military purpose against the United States." Fort Monroe quickly became known as "Freedom's Fortress." On May 27, Butler informed Winfield Scott that since 12 slaves had escaped from Sewell's Point to become contrabands, the value of ex-slaves in Union hands exceeded $60,000. "The negroes came pouring in day by day," Butler later wrote, "I found work for them to do, classified them and made a list of them so their identity might be fully assured, and appointed a 'commissioner of negro affairs' . . ." Eventually, several "contraband camps" were established, and the ex-slaves began to receive wages, as well as food and clothing, in return for work. Many contrabands became officers' servants or grew gardens and fished the bay to sell food to the soldiers. A few fortunate former bondsmen were able to join the U.S. Navy. The American Missionary Association (AMA) later organized several schools for the escaped slaves. Reverend Lewis C. Lockwood of the AMA noted with joy that the contrabands had "a great thirst for knowledge . . . parents and children are delighted with the idea of learning to read." Another missionary remembered passing by the "fortress chapel and adjacent yard, where most of the contraband tents are set . . . One young man sat on the end of a rude seat 'with a little book in the hand.' It had been much fingered, and he was stooping down towards the dim blaze of the fire, to make out the words . . . Where he had learned to read I know not, but where some of his companions will learn to read I do know."

Print by E. SACHSE & Cᵒ 104 S. Charles-st., Baltimore, Md.

ENCAMPMENT OF U. ST. TR

Butler's main objective, however, was not to free slaves, but to disrupt and capture any enemy batteries within a half day's march of Fort Monroe. He also wished to threaten the Confederate defenses on Craney Island and to recapture Gosport Navy Yard. The Confederates had already endeavored to counter Union control of Hampton Roads by erecting batteries at Sewell's Point, only 2.5 miles from the Rip Raps and 4 miles from Old Point Comfort. These fortifications defended the Elizabeth River approach to Norfolk and Portsmouth, while fortifications were built on Pig Point to control the entrance to the James River. Butler decided to contest the south side batteries and gain control of the James River by securing Newport News Point. On May 27, he sent three regiments of New York, Massachusetts, and Vermont volunteers with a detachment of U.S. Regulars and two 6-pound cannons on the steamer *Pawnee* to occupy

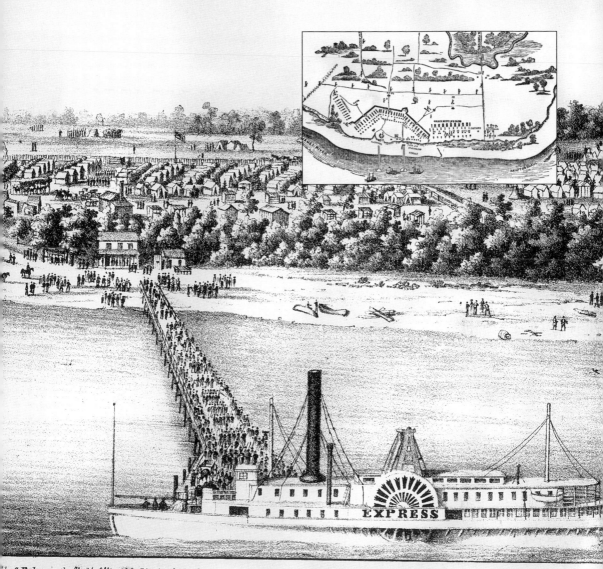

OPS AT NEWPORT NEWS, VA.

Newport News Point. Union forces landed without opposition and immediately began building an "entrenched camp." Butler believed that Newport News Point provided the Federals with numerous strategic opportunities. "The expedition to Newport News . . . landed without opposition," Butler advised Winfield Scott. "I have caused an entrenched camp to be made there, which, when completed, will be able to hold itself against any force that may be brought against it, and afford an even better depot from which to advance than Fortress Monroe." Butler also noted that the "advantages of the News are these: There are two springs of very pure water there; the bluff is a fine, healthy location. It has two good, commodious wharves, to which steamers of any draught may come up at all stages of the tide; it is as near any point of operation as Fortress Monroe . . . a force there is a perpetual threat to Richmond."

The Union position was named Camp Butler in honor of the department commander and soon became a major installation. "As soon as Colonel Phelps arrived, he began the erection of earthworks," Private William Osborne of the 4th Massachusetts recounted, "These were of semicircular form, terminating at either extremity on the bank of the river, and were nearly a half mile long. In the ditch in front of the works were placed obstructions . . . On the main works commanding the plain and forest were mounted a number of heavy guns, while on the bluff facing the river was a battery of five large pieces and among them a Sawyer and James rifle. Upon these works the men . . . labored for many days, and at a time when the weather was extremely hot." Butler viewed Camp Butler as a base from which he could operate against Suffolk, Norfolk, and Richmond.

When the 9th New York (Hawkins's Zouaves) arrived at Camp Butler on June 8, they found the 1st Vermont, 7th New York (an all German-speaking unit), and the Scott Life Guards camped within this fortified area. The earthwork extended over a mile protecting wharves, several buildings, and unit encampments. One Union soldier, Asher Williams, called the countryside beyond Camp Butler as "nothing more than a wild wilderness" and considered it as a "very dull place." Nevertheless, Williams wrote a friend the following: "You ask if there are any secesh here yes indeed in fact we are surrounded nothing but the river between us on three sides and North of us they are in large numbers at Yorktown and Great Bethel from our camp ground we can see their flag on Craney Island and also on Sewells point they have the impudence to come within a few miles of camp and take some of our men prisoners."

Butler realized that Castle Calhoun on the Rip Raps was only 2.5 miles from Sewell's Point and could be used to shell Confederate batteries guarding the entrance to the Elizabeth River. The stone fort still had two glaring weaknesses that would limit its effectiveness: the primary armaments and gun emplacements faced toward the Chesapeake Bay and the harbor entrance and the fort was still incomplete. Nevertheless, when Colonel Washington A. Barlett's Naval Brigade arrived on May 30, the unit was assigned to the Rip Raps. The Naval Brigade landed at night with the help of small boats from the USS *Cumberland*. Unfortunately, Colonel Barlett fell onto the rocks, grievously injuring himself. The Naval Brigade became disorganized, and the men were assigned as laborers until the unit was reorganized as the Union Coast Guard and the 99th New York Infantry. The 99th New York would eventually form Castle Calhoun's garrison.

The Naval Brigade had brought few weapons to Hampton Roads other than two rifled cannon. One of these, the Sawyer gun, greatly impressed General Butler and was mounted on the Rip Raps wharf by the *Cumberland*'s crew. This experimental gun was invented by Sylvanus Sawyer and fired a lead-coated shell with six ribs cast to its exterior to fit the weapon's rifling. Although other versions of the Sawyer gun were prone to bursting and the gun was difficult to load, the 24-pounder model on the Rip Raps could shell Sewell's Point with some accuracy. Butler ordered Fort Monroe's ordnance workshop to rifle two more 6-pounders to take the elongated Sawyer shell.

Butler made an effort to strengthen Fort Monroe's armaments. On June 14, the massive 12-inch, 52,005-pound "Union Gun" arrived. This giant rifled gun fired a shell weighing from 360 to 420 pounds over 4 miles, but it proved to be extremely difficult to transport. The 15-inch smoothbore Rodman gun, which would later be remounted and renamed the Lincoln Gun, weighed 49,100 pounds and could hurl a projectile 5,375 yards, making it the largest gun in the United States in 1861. It was invented by Captain Thomas J. Rodman, and even though a success, it was soon made obsolete by the development of rifled artillery.

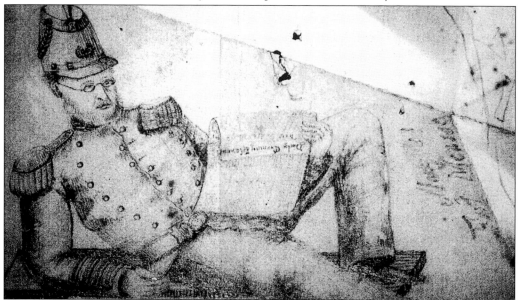

The Union's ability to maintain control of Fort Monroe during the secession crisis provided the nation with an important strategic and symbolic toehold in Confederate territory. There was little the Confederates could do to contest the Union bastion on Old Point Comfort because of the U.S. Navy's ability to resupply Fort Monroe via the Chesapeake Bay. The Federals had demonstrated by their march into Hampton and occupation of Newport News Point during May 1861 that they had the strength to advance anywhere on the Peninsula. The certainty of that power is reflected in the relaxed attitude of this officer of the 3rd Massachusetts, drawn in June 1861. Butler believed that he could continue to expand the Federal presence throughout the Hampton Roads region.

Four

"HE DIED NOBLY FIGHTING HIS GUNS"

The rapid expansion of Union power on the lower Peninsula in late May alarmed the commander of the Provisional Army of Virginia, Robert E. Lee. Federal reinforcements, like these officers of the 10th New York, continued to arrive at Fort Monroe. Lee recognized the Union build-up on the Peninsula as an immediate threat against Norfolk and Richmond. Consequently, Lee sent Colonel John Bankhead Magruder to assume command at Yorktown and organize Confederate defenses. Magruder surveyed the Peninsula and decided to build his primary line of defense across the Peninsula from Mulberry Island on the James River and follow the Warwick River to Yorktown on the York River. However, he needed time and men to prepare this defensive line against any concerted Union advance. Magruder was reinforced in late May with cavalry commanded by John Bell Hood and the 1st North Carolina Volunteers commanded by D.H. Hill. He selected Big Bethel Church as the site to provoke Butler into an attack.

This new Confederate stance was immediately countered by the Federals. Union patrols ranged farther into the countryside surrounding Fort Monroe. On June 4, a contingent of the 5th New York marched to the small village of Fox Hill 5 miles away from the fort. Their mission was to retrieve men from the 1st New York purportedly captured by Confederate pickets. The Federals did not find any evidence of Confederate activity at Fox Hill and continued their forced march another 5 miles to the Back River. The New Yorkers began their return to Fort Monroe by way of Hampton when a courier arrived with news that the 1st New York was safe. En route to the fort, one Union officer, Lieutenant Burnett, was shot in the chest with a spent ball. This minor injury was the expedition's only casualty.

On June 6, 1861, Major Edgar B. Montague was ordered by Magruder to establish an advanced position at Big Bethel Church with three companies of Virginia volunteers. Big Bethel was a small crossroads on the Hampton-York Highway 8 miles from Hampton and located at a bend in the northwestern branch (known as Brick Kiln Creek) of the Back River. D.H. Hill's 1st North Carolina reinforced Big Bethel the next day. Additional units were also sent to Bethel, including Major George Wythe Randolph's Richmond Howitzers and Lieutenant Colonel W.D. Stuart's command of four companies of the 15th Virginia Infantry. D.H. Hill exercised command of this force of 1,458 men. Hill established a forward position 3 miles away at Little Bethel and fortified Big Bethel with a series of redoubts. J.W. Ratchford, an aide to D.H. Hill, noted the Confederates' precarious position, "It looked as if Magruder was only sending us down to the vicinity of the fort as a dare to General Benjamin F. Butler. He no doubt thought we had sense enough to get out of the way."

On June 9, Butler learned about the increasing Confederate force at Big Bethel, which threatened the land communications between Camp Butler and Fort Monroe. Butler was convinced that he must strike out and destroy the Confederate outpost at Little Bethel and fortifications at Big Bethel. The Union general thought that such an action might even open the door for an advance against Richmond. Accordingly, a rather complex plan was devised by Butler's military secretary, Major Theodore Winthrop, to dispatch troops from Camp Butler, Camp Hamilton, and Fort Monroe to converge on Big Bethel at dawn on June 10. Winthrop believed that a night march would give the Union force an element of surprise that, it was hoped, would help ensure victory. Winthrop even took steps to avoid any confusion caused by the junction of various units near Bethel in the darkness. Federal soldiers wore white armbands to distinguish themselves from the enemy. In addition, the password "Boston" was used when unrecognized troops approached each other en route to Bethel.

The entire operation, numbering 4,400 men, was placed under the command of Brigadier General Ebenezer W. Pierce, commander of Camp Hamilton. Duryee's Zouaves led the march from Camp Hamilton at midnight to intersect the Confederate positions between Little and Big Bethel. The Zouaves were then followed one hour later by Colonel Frank Townsend's 3rd New York Regiment with two howitzers. Lieutenant Colonel Peter T. Washburn organized a battalion of volunteers from the 1st Vermont and 4th Massachusetts, who were to march from Camp Butler in front of Little Bethel. Colonel John E. Bendix's 7th New York was to follow Washburn from Newport News Point. The plan dictated that Bendix and Townsend should juncture near Little Bethel and then march on the Confederate positions. Elements of Duryee's Zouaves, led by Captain Judson Kilpatrick, captured three Confederate pickets before dawn and were in position to continue their advance. Unfortunately, other parts of the Union advance did not proceed as planned. As the 3rd New York approached the 7th New York in the darkness, Bendix's men, unable to see the white armbands and alerted by the sound of horses, nervously fired into the ranks of the 3rd New York before Townsend's troops could identify themselves. This alerted the Confederates, and they abandoned Little Bethel to make a more resolute stand at Big Bethel. The Federals suffered 18 casualties. General Pierce hastily convened a council of war and proceeded with the attack.

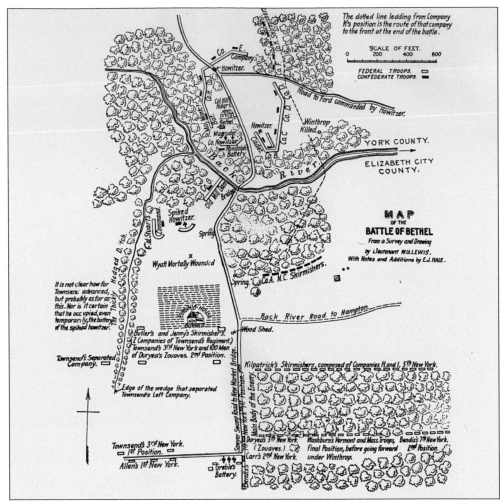

The dotted line leading from Company H's position is the route of that company to the front at the end of the battle.

SCALE OF FEET.
0   200   400   600

FEDERAL TROOPS.
CONFEDERATE TROOPS.

Road to Ford commanded by Howitzer.

YOR'K COUNTY.

ELIZABETH CITY COUNTY.

MAP
OF THE
BATTLE OF BETHEL
From a Survey and Drawing
by Lieutenant W.H.LEWIS.
With Notes and Additions by E.J. HALE.

Back River Road to Hampton.

As the Federals reorganized themselves, the Confederates prepared to defend their entrenchment. Men of the 3rd Virginia, along with one howitzer, manned the redoubt on the southern side of Brick Kiln Creek. Sharpshooters from the 1st North Carolina were posted along the edge of the woods of the Hampton-York Highway. On the northern side of Brick Kiln Creek, the Richmond Howitzers were positioned in the main redoubt guarding the bridge with three guns. Major Montague's companies and elements of the 1st North Carolina held the flanks and rear of the main redoubt.

The Union force was rather disorganized when they arrived on the field, and units attacked in a piecemeal fashion. Kilpatrick led Duryee's Zouaves on the first assault around 9:00 a.m. This advance pushed aside the Confederate pickets, but was quickly stopped by accurate artillery fire. The Zouaves, suffering severe casualties, fell back behind an orchard. A Union artillery battery arrived in position under the command of Lieutenant John T. Greble. An artillery duel between Greble's guns and Randolph's howitzers ensued.

Meanwhile, a second attack was organized. The 3rd New York moved to envelop the Confederate right as the 5th New York and 2nd New York moved across the field toward the redoubt. The 15th Virginia abandoned their position when the howitzer malfunctioned. The New Yorkers, personally led by Abram Duryee, pressed the Confederates, but a move by the Zouaves to cross an old ford downstream was blocked by a company of the 3rd Virginia, which had just fallen back across the creek.

46

Simultaneously, Colonel Townsend began to urge his men to assault the Confederate right when he noticed a glint of bayonets reflecting in the sun through the woods. Thinking that his troops were about to be flanked by a Confederate force, Townsend ordered a withdrawal. This left the Zouaves isolated in the Confederate redoubt. Under pressure from a counterattack by men from the 3rd Virginia, Wythe Rifles, and the 1st North Carolina, they retreated.

When the Federals fell back from the advance redoubt, Major Theodore Winthrop organized an assault on the Confederate left using Vermont and Massachusetts troops. Winthrop led his men across the creek with a cheer and advanced toward the main redoubt under a withering fire. In an effort to rally his men for a final charge that might have carried the day for the Union, Winthrop stood up on a log waving his sword. He was immediately shot through the heart and fell dead onto the ground. His death completely demoralized his troops, and they fell back across Brick Kiln Creek. This retreat, wrote D.H. Hill, "decided the action in our favor."

The action at the masked [...] Capt [...] [...] 2nd [...] [...] taking charge of the [...] [...] Great Bethel. Death of Lieut. Greble of Phil [...] the enemy.

Big Bethel was a complete failure for the Union. The Federals lost a total of 76 men: 18 killed, 53 wounded, and 5 missing. Butler was blamed for ordering his troops into battle with poor intelligence and for remaining at Fort Monroe during the engagement. Pierce, however, received most of the blame for the Union disaster. The *New York Times* noted that Pierce "lost his presence of mind" during the battle. He was labeled incompetent and was mustered out of the Army after his 90-day enlistment. The Northern press tried to salvage some honor out of the defeat. The Union troops were called courageous as "they fought both friend and foe alike with equal resolution and only retired after exhausting their ammunition in face of a powerful enemy."

Theodore Winthrop and John T. Greble (pictured here), who was killed near the end of the battle while "nobly fighting his guns," were lionized for their valor and sacrifice. Lieutenant Greble was the first Regular Army officer and West Point graduate killed during the war. He had commanded his battery with distinction during the battle and was described as possessing "to a notable degree the two qualities most needed at the time, namely, military skill and presence of mind in face of the enemy." Major Winthrop was, according to D.H. Hill, the "only one of the enemy who exhibited an approximation of courage that day." Winthrop, who was told by Butler to "Be Bold! Be Bold! But not too bold," almost won the day for the Union with his bravery. Several articles he had penned about his service in Virginia were posthumously published by the *Atlantic Monthly*, which earned Winthrop even greater fame for his fateful heroism at Big Bethel.

During the weeks following Big Bethel, the two opposing forces continued to probe the land between Big Bethel and Fort Monroe. Butler sent two expeditions from Fort Monroe on June 24 to harass the Confederates. The first was just a demonstration near Big Bethel; however, the other expedition had a greater mission. Elements of the 10th New York marched from Fort Monroe to the mouth of the Back River, where they met the steamers *Adriatic* and *Fanny* and a steam launch from the USS *Roanoke*. The New Yorkers were then transported upstream to destroy vessels from the Eastern Shore laden with supplies for nearby Confederate troops. A total of 14 sailing ships and numerous small boats were destroyed on the Back River and Harris Creek. The Confederates endeavored to strike back at the marauding Federals. Several skirmishes occurred along the Great Warwick Road as the Confederates tried to trap Union foraging expeditions operating from Camp Butler.

The Federal defeat during the Battle of Bull Run on July 21, 1861, forced Winfield Scott to order Butler to send 4,000 soldiers from Fort Monroe to help defend Washington, D.C. This troop reduction forced Butler to abandon Hampton on July 25, and to restrict troop movement to established encampments. The Federal evacuation of Hampton prompted Magruder to increase the pressure on the virtually isolated Camp Butler. On July 28, Magruder sent a flag of truce to Camp Butler demanding that the Federals leave Newport News Point or be assaulted. He continued to demonstrate in front of the Union entrenchments hoping to draw the Federals into battle.

Butler realized that his communication with the outlying posts could be severed by the Confederates. He had already installed a telegraph line connecting Fort Monroe with Camp Hamilton and Camp Butler; however, Butler was still concerned about his lack of knowledge of Confederate troop movements. Butler had already arranged for the acclaimed aeronaut, John LaMountain, to serve the Union Department of Virginia as an aerial observer. LaMountain (pictured here) arrived on July 23, and on July 31 he completed his first successful flight on the Peninsula, reaching an altitude of 1,400 feet and observing a radius of over 30 miles. Another flight on August 1 discovered the Confederate camp at Young's Mill. LaMountain estimated that over 4,000 soldiers were stationed at Young's Mill and another 500 held an advanced position on Water's Creek.

On August 3, 1861, LaMountain made his first flight from the deck of the gunboat *Fanny*. The *Fanny*, with LaMountain's balloon secured to the ship's deck with a windlass and mooring ropes, steamed into the channel off Sewell's Point. The balloon reached a height of 2,000 feet and enabled a thorough inspection of the Confederate positions defending Norfolk. LaMountain provided Butler with this sketch of the Confederate position at Sewell's Point after his second flight from the deck of the tug *Adriatic* and advised the Union commander that he could "shell, burn or destroy Norfolk."

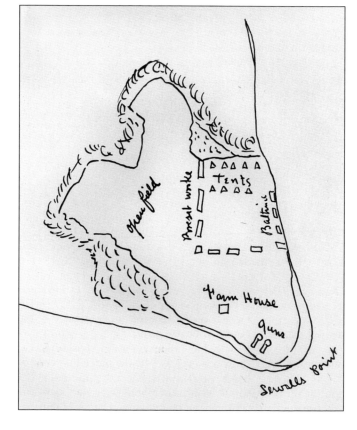

LaMountain's aerial reconnaissance did not observe Magruder's large force of 4,000 infantry, 400 cavalry, and the Richmond Howitzers move against Camp Butler on August 6. Magruder penetrated the Union lines, cut the telegraph line, and marched within a mile of Hampton. During his march toward Hampton, Magruder obtained a copy of a *New York Tribune* that contained a report from Butler to Secretary of War Simon Cameron stating that the Union general planned to colonize the numerous contrabands in Hampton, "the home of most of their owners." Magruder, realizing that he could not hold Hampton because of its proximity to Fort Monroe, decided to destroy the town. The Confederate general organized a strike force under the command of local resident Captain Jefferson Curle Phillips of the Old Dominion Dragoons to complete this "loathsome yet patriotic act." Consequently, after dark on August 7, 1861, Phillips ordered that each company would fire one quarter of the town as divided at the cross streets. They immediately went to work. "Flames were seen bursting from the buildings on all sides till it appeared that the town was one mass of flames."

When the Confederates left Hampton burning, "there rested in the hearts of each of us the realization of a great sacrifice nobly made," wrote Robert Hudgins of the Old Dominion Dragoons. The Federals, however, were shocked by Hampton's destruction; one Northern newspaper called it "a wanton act of cruelty to the resident Unionists, and moreover useless." "Such a picture of war and desolation I never saw nor thought of, and hope I shall not again," wrote Lieutenant Charles Harvey Brewster, "I pass through the churchyard round the celebrated Hampton Church, the oldest one in use in the United States, it is completely destroyed and all but the walls and they are useless." It was indeed an eerie scene, as one Union correspondent noted, "Nothing but a forest of black sided chimneys and walls of brick houses tottering and cooling in the wind, scorched and seared trees and heaps of smoldering ruins mark the site . . . . A more desolate sight cannot be imagined than is Hampton today."

Ben Butler could not understand the Confederate scorched earth policy. He wrote to officials in Washington that a "more wanton and unnecessary act than the burning could not have been committed. I confess myself so poor a soldier as not to be able to discern the strategic importance of this movement." Butler believed that Hampton's destruction signified that the war was now entering a new phase. "This act upon the part of the enemy seems to me to be a representative one," Butler wrote Winfield Scott, "showing the spirit in which the war is to be carried on on their part, and which perhaps will have a tendency to provoke a corresponding spirit on our part, but we may hope not."

Butler had already had misgivings about his command of such a difficult and critical arena of war as Hampton Roads. On July 29, he traveled to Washington to discuss with Winfield Scott the need to assign an experienced, high-ranking regular as commander of the Union Department of Virginia. Scott ordered Major General John Ellis Wool on August 8 to assume command at Fort Monroe and assigned Butler to command all volunteer regiments outside of the fort.

Five

WOOL AND THE CAROLINAS

On August 17, 1861, Fort Monroe came under the command of John Ellis Wool, one of the Army's most distinguished officers. Born in 1784 in Troy, New York, Wool joined the Army with the start of the War of 1812, was appointed a captain in the 13th Infantry, and fought bravely at the battles of Queenstown Heights and Plattsburgh. He was brevetted to the ranks of major and lieutenant colonel and was assigned to the 29th U.S. Infantry. Rising to the rank of colonel, he became the U.S. Army's Inspector General in 1816, and was promoted to brigadier general in 1841. During the Mexican War, he served as General Zachary Taylor's second in command at the Battle of Buena Vista; for his conduct he was promoted to brevet major general, voted the thanks of Congress, and awarded a sword. Just prior to the Civil War, he was appointed to the command of the Military Department of the East. He ensured that Fort Monroe, which he saw as the "key to all the states South," was kept for the Union by reinforcing its garrison with militia regiments from his department. The oldest officer on either side of the conflict to hold an active command during the war, General Wool brought with him much needed experience in military affairs.

FORTRESS MONROE   RIP RAPS.

HYGEIA

THE GREAT EXPEDITION._THE VE
FROM THE TOP OF THE HYG

Under General Wool's command, Fort Monroe became the center of several important activities taking place in Southeast Virginia and the coastal Carolinas. Shortly after Wool's arrival, General Butler gathered a force of nearly 900 men from the fort and embarked them on naval vessels under the command of Silas H. Stringham. The object of the expedition was Hatteras Island, about 140 miles below Norfolk. Hatteras is located in a prominent position by an entrance to both the Albemarle and Pamlico Sounds, but is most closely situated to control the latter. These large bodies of shallow water became very important to the Confederacy in negating the direct blockade of both Norfolk and Richmond. Acting as a "back door" for these cities, shallow draft, fast-moving ships could move quickly through the area, keeping open trade in spite of the blockade. Commerce raiders also operated from these waters. This first amphibious expedition would regain control of this area for the Union. The fleet left Hampton Roads on August 26, and Hatteras Island's fortifications were quickly subdued by naval bombardment. The troops landed and took possession of the forts on the 29th. The area was soon reinforced with more soldiers, also from the department at Fort Monroe.

By early October 1861, the Union was ready to extend its control farther along the Confederate coast. The objective this time was Port Royal, South Carolina. A fine, large harbor, its possession

S AT ANCHOR AT HAMPTON ROADS,
OTEL, OLD POINT COMFORT, VA.

would provide the Union Navy with a good station to operate from and extend the range of the blockading squadron. The Confederates also recognized the value of this port with its proximity to Savannah and Charleston. They had prepared its defense with two strong forts named Walker and Beauregard. The forts were on each side of the harbor entrance and each mounted dozens of heavy guns. The Union task force, under Flag Officer Samuel F. DuPont, assembled at Hampton Roads, just off Fort Monroe. It was the largest U.S. Navy flotilla assembled at that time. It carried a landing force of 17,000 soldiers under Brigadier General Thomas W. Sherman. The objective of the expedition was kept secret and a cause for speculation among the fort's population. As one of the wives living at the fort wrote to her nephew, "Indeed, if you were here and could see the immense array of ships in the harbor prepared to do battle, you would be Yankee enough to 'guess' it was 'war time.' I am told that there was never so large a fleet of war ships in our waters before. There is an expedition fitting our here of a great number of vessels, but their destination is unknown even to their commanders. They probably have sealed orders, and if numbers will make them successful, I think they must surely be so."

The expedition left Hampton Roads on October 29. The fleet ran into a great storm while at sea off Cape Hatteras. While the armada was dispersed for several days, most of the ships managed to reform off Port Royal, having suffered little loss of life. The action opened on November 7. A flanking squadron was sent ahead to drive back the small Confederate flotilla operating in Port Royal Sound and keep it from interfering with the operation. Flag Officer Samuel DuPont then sailed the vessels of his main fleet in line into the harbor entrance, within 600 yards of Fort Walker. As each ship bombarded the fort in turn, they proceeded into the harbor, turned, and came back along the other side to bombard Fort Beauregard. Catching the forts at point-blank range along their less protected northern sides, the Union fire was accurate and deadly. The fleet's 155 guns showered shells on the Confederate fortifications "as fast," one Union officer recounted, "as a horse's feet beat the ground in a gallop." After three such evolutions, most of the forts' 43 guns were dismounted. The Confederate defenders abandoned Fort Walker early in the afternoon, and a portion of Brigadier General Thomas W. Sherman's 12,000 troops were quickly landed to take possession. At sunset, Fort Beauregard also hauled its flag down, and the Union Army soon occupied this second fort. Due to this highly successful operation, Port Royal and neighboring Hilton Head Island became important bases for the Union Army and Navy for the remainder of the war. Port Royal Sound quickly became a major base for the U.S. Navy's blockading operations along the coast of South Carolina, Georgia, and Florida. Equally important to the war's history, the large plantations of this portion of the coast came under Union control, along with their large slave population. Soon, the sea islands of South Carolina became the site of missionary activity, as earnest teachers from the North arrived to educate these newly freed bondsmen.

The interest of the Union Navy in controlling the coast of the Carolinas turned next to Roanoke Island in North Carolina. The Hatteras Island expedition had already cut off the use of Pamlico Sound to privateers and blockade-runners. Now the Navy planned to extend control throughout the Albemarle Sound as well. Brigadier General Ambrose Burnside was placed in charge of the Army's portion of this joint expedition. A full corps of three divisions was assembled at Annapolis, and then shipped to Fort Monroe on January 8, 1862. There, they rendezvoused with the warships and transports of a fleet commanded by Flag Officer Louis M. Goldsborough. The fleet sailed out of the Virginia Capes on January 11 and 12, heading south.

"Roanoke Island is ours!," wrote a triumphant Federal soldier from Rhode Island to his parents on February 11, 1862. The light-draft warships of the Union fleet had chased off Confederate vessels and bombarded the fort and batteries guarding the island. The Federal troops landed on the western side of the island, and slogged forward through tidal marsh and Confederate fire. As they moved inland, they guided along a road through the marsh, which was defended by a three-gun Confederate battery. One Union regiment advanced along each side of the road, but it was slow going. Finally, the 9th New York Infantry (Hawkins's Zouaves) formed up and charged along the road. They rushed over the Confederate work, driving off the surviving defenders. Soon the entire island was in Union hands. "It now requires no farreaching prophet," Horace Greeley wrote, "to predict the end of this struggle." The *Richmond Examiner* lamented the loss of Roanoke Island as "certainly the most painful event of the war." With the capture of Roanoke, the Union was ready to begin a series of operations against Confederate coastal cities, such as New Bern, Beaufort, and Fort Macon. Federal control of Roanoke Island and the Carolina Sounds also provided an opportunity to strike against the critical railroad link between Richmond and the blockade runners' haven of Wilmington, North Carolina. In addition, Richmond was deprived of a close area for the operation of blockade runners and important foodstuffs produced in this fertile region. Control of this area also gave the Union another avenue of approach for the possible recapture of Norfolk and the Gosport Navy Yard.

The work of improving the fort's armament, which had begun just before the start of the war, was continued with the experiments of General Butler and also under General Wool. Of all the types of guns experimented with by Butler, the Rodmans were the ones that would be brought into the fort in the greatest numbers. Various calibers of Rodmans were emplaced on

the ramparts or along the beach and mounted in different carriages. This photograph shows a group of officers of the Ordnance Corps, led by the chief of ordnance, Brigadier General A.B. Dyer (number 1 in the photograph), at Fort Monroe on an inspection tour in 1864.

This print shows the most famous of all the guns that formed part of the fort's armament during the Civil War. Cast in 1860 at the Fort Pitt Foundry, it has a bore of 15 inches and weighs 49,099 pounds. Originally named for President Buchanan's secretary of war, John B. Floyd, it was sent to Fort Monroe in 1860 and fired 509 test rounds with varying charges of powder and at different elevations. Its greatest recorded range was 5,730 yards (over 3 miles) with a 40-pound powder charge at 28° 35' elevation. It could fire either a solid shot of 450 pounds or a shell of 330 pounds. It was estimated that at an elevation of 39° and a 40-pound charge, it would exceed a range of 4 miles. Following the battle between the *Monitor* and the *Merrimack* (the *Virginia*), General Wool ordered this gun, now renamed the Lincoln Gun, to be mounted on the beach near the Union Gun, a 12-inch rifled Rodman. A special platform of stone was built to hold the gun on a new carriage of cast iron and oak. Both the Lincoln and Union Guns were fired on April 15 and 16 toward the Confederate fortifications at Sewell's Point, near Norfolk. The fall of that city to Union forces on May 11, 1862, ended the Lincoln Gun's active service.

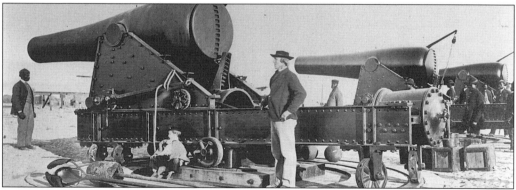

Rodman guns represented the height of black powder, smoothbore, muzzle-loading artillery technology. The design was a radical departure from previous methods of casting guns, in which unequal rates of cooling of the inside and outside of the metal caused structural flaws. Captain Thomas J. Rodman cast his guns around a solid core and cooled them with a jet of water inside and out. The stronger metal that resulted allowed for larger guns of 8-, 10-, 12-, 15-, and even 20-inch bore to be manufactured. Captain Rodman also invented a new hexagonal powder, called "Mammoth Powder," which helped to increase the gun's range. Throughout the war, many of these Rodman guns in various calibers were brought to the fort. They were often placed on experimental, cast-iron carriages, such as those pictured here. These carriages show a pneumatic buffer that would absorb the force of the recoil and the cranes needed to lift the 330 to 450 pound balls so they could be loaded at the cannon's muzzle. By 1865, there were 66 of this type of gun at Fort Monroe. They would remain the major portion of the fort's armament up to the Spanish-American War.

Six

LINCOLN AND THE FALL OF NORFOLK

When Major General George Brinton
McClellan assumed command of the
demoralized Army of the Potomac
following the Bull Run disaster, he
quickly transformed the Union Army
into the most powerful army ever
witnessed in America. McClellan
provided his troops with the best
training, armaments, and organization
then known to military service. The
35-year-old major general replaced the
aged Winfield Scott as general-in-chief of
the Union Army and seemed destined for
success. Yet by late 1861, McClellan had
not made any effort to assault the nearby
Confederate Army at Manassas. President
Abraham Lincoln pressed McClellan
into developing some plan to attack
the Confederate capital in Richmond.
McClellan sought to avoid marching
overland toward Richmond, which he
believed would result in extensive Union
casualties. Instead, the Union general
purposed a move to strike Richmond
by way of Urbanna, located on the
Rappahannock River.

Before McClellan could execute his plan, General Joseph E. Johnston pulled his army from Manassas to Fredericksburg on March 7, 1862. Johnston's retreat ruined the Urbanna Plan's prospects, and McClellan immediately put forth his secondary concept. McClellan thought that by "using Fort Monroe as a base," the Army of the Potomac could march against Richmond "with complete security, altho' with less celerity and brilliancy of results, up the Peninsula." McClellan's plan was a sound strategic concept, as it employed a shrewd exploitation of Union naval superiority: gunboats could protect his flanks and transports could carry his troops up the James and York Rivers toward the Confederate capital.

As McClellan shared the merits of his plan with Lincoln and strove to allay the President's fears for the defense of Washington, his campaign started to unhinge. The emergence of the powerful ironclad ram CSS *Virginia* into Hampton Roads on March 8, 1862, sent shockwaves through the Union command. The *Virginia* was converted from the USS *Merrimack*, scuttled when the Federal forces evacuated Norfolk in 1861. The ironclad was plated with 4 inches of iron and armed with ten guns. In one day, the *Virginia* destroyed two Union warships, the USS *Congress* and USS *Cumberland*, off Newport News Point and threatened Federal control of Hampton Roads. President Lincoln viewed the March 8, 1862 events as the greatest Union calamity since Bull Run. Secretary of War Edwin W. Stanton feared that the *Virginia* "would soon come up the Potomac and dispose Congress, destroy the Capitol and public buildings . . . ." Stanton truly believed that "McClellan's mistaken purpose to advance the Peninsula must be abandoned."

As the burning *Congress* sent an eerie glow across the harbor on the evening of March 8, the USS *Monitor* arrived in Hampton Roads. It had almost sunk en route from New York. The *Monitor* was a completely new concept of naval design, created by Swedish inventor John Ericsson. Its revolving turret housed two 11-inch Dahlgrens, and the ironclad's decks were virtually awash with the sea. On the morning of March 9, 1862, the Confederate ironclad steamed back into Hampton Roads from Sewell's Point to complete the destruction of the wooden Union fleet. The *Virginia*'s crew was surprised to see the "cheesebox on a raft" approach their vessel and block their path to a stranded frigate, the USS *Minnesota*. For the next two hours the *Monitor* and *Virginia* dueled, but neither ship was able to inflict serious damage on the other. The *Monitor* briefly broke off the engagement to resupply ammunition. The *Virginia* took this opportunity to move against the *Minnesota*, but ran aground. The *Virginia* somehow was able to free herself and then tried to ram the *Monitor*. The collision caused more damage to the Confederate vessel, as the *Virginia*'s wooden hull glanced off the iron deck of the more nimble *Monitor*. When the Union ironclad tried to ram the *Virginia*'s rudder, a shell struck the *Monitor*'s pilothouse, blinding her commander, Lieutenant John Lorimer Worden, and causing the *Monitor* to temporarily break off action. Believing that the Union ironclad had had enough and suffering from several leaks, the *Virginia* returned to Norfolk with the receding tide.

Both sides claimed victory. The *Monitor* was successful in stopping the Confederate ironclad from destroying the Federal fleet. The *Virginia*, however, blocked the James River and closed this approach to the Union fleet. A few days after the battle McClellan inquired of the U.S. Navy whether or not he could "rely on the *Monitor* to keep the *Merrimack* in check, so that I can make Fort Monroe a base of operations?" Gustavus Vasa Fox, assistant secretary of the navy, replied that the "*Monitor* is more than a match for the *Merrimack*, but she might be disabled in the next encounter . . . The *Monitor* may, and I think will, destroy the *Merrimack* in the next fight; but this is hope not certainty . . . ." McClellan was concerned. "The performances of the *Merrimac* place a new aspect upon everything," McClellan wrote General Wool, "and may very probably change my whole plan of campaign, just on the eve of execution."

Even though many Union officers, such as Brigadier General John G. Barnard, believed that the "possibility of the *Merrimack* appearing again paralyzes the movement of this Army," McClellan was confident that the *Monitor* could protect his army's transports and decided to proceed with his campaign. He began shipping his huge army, which was larger than the population of any city in Virginia, on March 17, 1862. The first divisions, Brigadier General Samuel P. Heintzelman's III Corps, landed at Fort Monroe on March 18. By early April, McClellan had assembled the entire Army of the Potomac on the tip of the Peninsula, including 121,500 men, 1,150 wagons, 44 batteries, 103 siege guns, 74 ambulances, pontoon bridges, telegraph equipment, "and the enormous quantity of equipage . . . required for an army of such magnitude." McClellan intended to use this massive force to move against Richmond by way of the York River. McClellan advised Lincoln that he intended "to take the field immediately upon arriving at Fort Monroe . . . by rapid movements to drive before me, or capture the enemy on the peninsula, open the James River, and push on to Richmond before he could be materially reinforced from other portions of his territory . . . ."

All of McClellan's previous delays prompted Lincoln to relieve McClellan as general-in-chief of the entire Union Army, forcing him to focus on the Army of the Potomac's march against Richmond. McClellan arrived on the Peninsula in early April and immediately sought to place Fort Monroe's garrison under his control. This action resulted in a minor feud with General Wool (pictured at left). The 78-year-old Wool believed that since he had been made a brevet major general in the Mexican War, he outranked McClellan and, accordingly, thought that the younger officer should be subject to his orders. This circumstance caused some awkwardness between the two generals and prompted McClellan, who was the senior regular major general in the Army, to ignore Wool's advice about the Confederate troop dispositions on the Peninsula.

Wool had employed spies to glean information about the Confederate defenses on the Peninsula. A soldier was ordered to desert and join the Confederate Army and discover everything there was to know about the Yorktown defenses. Wool secured this information and then provided McClellan with an estimated Confederate troop strength of 15,000 men as well as "precise information of the rebel works between York and James Rivers." The troop strength was accurate; however, the information about Confederate fortifications would eventually prove to be misleading.

Since the CSS *Virginia* blocked the James River, McClellan planned to outflank the Confederates at their Yorktown defenses; thereby, forcing a Confederate retreat. Allan Pinkerton, the famous detective, reported that the Confederate right flank was unsecured. The Federal commander thought that he could interpose his troops across the Confederate line of retreat, trapping Major General John Bankhead Magruder's Army of the Peninsula at Yorktown like George Washington had cornered Lord Cornwallis in 1781. Maps provided by General Wool indicated good roads and no water barriers, so McClellan seemed sure of a quick victory on the lower Peninsula, which would open the door to Richmond's capture.

The Union Army began its march on April 4, 1862. Brigadier General Samuel Peter Heintzelman's III Corps and Brigadier General Edwin Vose Sumner's II Corps marched up the Hampton-York Highway through Big Bethel to Yorktown. Meanwhile, Brigadier General Erasmus Darwin Keyes's IV Corps moved up the Great Warwick Road through Young's Mill en route to the Half-Way House to block Magruder's retreat from Yorktown. The Union troops occupied both Big Bethel and Young's Mill on April 4 without any bloodshed, and McClellan's plan appeared destined for success. The next day, the Army of the Potomac resumed its march only to find its path slowed by heavy rains, which turned the already poor roads into a muddy morass. His army then was blocked by Magruder's small army entrenched along a 12-mile front between the James River and Yorktown.

Brigadier General John G. Barnard, the Army of the Potomac's chief engineer, called the comprehensive series of redoubts and rifle pits arrayed behind the flooded Warwick River "one of the most extensive known to modern times." General Keyes concurred and believed that no "part of this line as discovered can be taken without an enormous waste of life." The Union Army halted in its tracks as Magruder, despite being heavily outnumbered, created an illusion of a powerful army. He "played his ten thousand before McClellan like fireflies," wrote diarist Mary Chesnut, "and utterly deluded him." "The assuming and maintaining of the line by Magruder, with his small force in face of such overwhelming odds," wrote Brigadier General Jubal A. Early, "was one of the boldest exploits ever performed by a military commander . . . ." Indeed, Prince John Magruder earned his title of the "Master of Ruses and Strategy" for his desperate, yet dramatic, ruse of strength that baffled the Union Army commander along the Warwick River.

The events of April 5, 1862, disrupted McClellan's campaign. His plans for a rapid movement to capture Yorktown were foiled by the unexpected Confederate defenses. In addition, Lincoln refused to send McClellan reinforcements, and the U.S. Navy refused to attack the Confederate York River water batteries. Since McClellan's reconnaissance, provided by detective Allan Pinkerton and Professor Thaddeus Lowe's balloons, confirmed his belief that he was outnumbered by the Confederates, he besieged their defenses. As McClellan's men built gun emplacements for the 103 siege guns he brought to the Peninsula, General Joseph E. Johnston began moving his entire Confederate army to the lower Peninsula. Johnston thought the Confederate position weak, noting that "no one but McClellan could have hesitated to attack." Johnston advised that "the fight for Yorktown must be one of artillery, in which we cannot win. The result is certain; the time only doubtful."

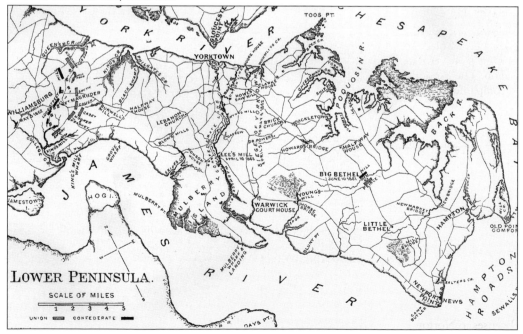

Johnston counseled retreat. Consequently, on the evening of May 3, just as McClellan made his last preparations to begin his heavy bombardment of Yorktown, the Confederates abandoned their fortifications. Even though he was surprised by the Confederate withdrawal, McClellan immediately attempted to cut off Johnston's retreat. The result was the bloody, indecisive Battle of Williamsburg on May 5, 1862. The battle was fought along the Williamsburg Line, a series of 14 redoubts built by the Confederates between Queen's and College Creeks. The Union Army was able to capture several redoubts at the end of the battle; however, the Confederate Army was able to continue its retreat toward Richmond.

Abraham Lincoln, dismayed by the inaction of McClellan and the U.S. Navy, decided to go to Fort Monroe to prompt more resolute action. The President, accompanied by Brigadier General Egbert L. Viele, Secretary of the Treasury Salmon P. Chase, and Secretary of War Edwin M. Stanton, arrived at the Engineer's Wharf on board the U.S. revenue cutter *Miami* during the evening of May 6, 1862. The President had been invited to Fort Monroe by General Wool in conjunction with Wool's plans to strike against the Confederate defenses in Norfolk.

Since McClellan's forces were already moving up the Peninsula toward Richmond, Lincoln focused on Norfolk and the CSS *Virginia*. A council of war was held in Fort Monroe's Old Quarters No. 1 (pictured here) with General Wool and Flag Officer Louis M. Goldsborough. Accordingly, Lincoln ordered Goldsborough to simultaneously send a naval strike force up the James River and shell Sewell's Point, silencing the Confederate batteries.

On May 8, Goldsborough sent the USS *Monitor* and the iron-hulled USS *Naugatuck*, supported by several wooden warships including the USS *Susquehanna* and USS *San Jacinto*, against the Sewell's Point batteries. Shortly after the shelling began, the CSS *Virginia* steamed down the Elizabeth River to attack the Union vessels. While it appeared that a second battle between the *Monitor* and *Virginia* might occur, Goldsborough commanded the Federal ships to withdraw to their anchorage beyond Fort Monroe. The CSS *Virginia* steamed around Hampton Roads for the next two hours and then returned to its base. One of the *Virginia*'s crew, John Taylor Wood, noted that the *Monitor*'s refusal to combat the Confederate ironclad "was the most cowardly exhibition I have ever seen . . . Goldsborough and Jeffers are two cowards."

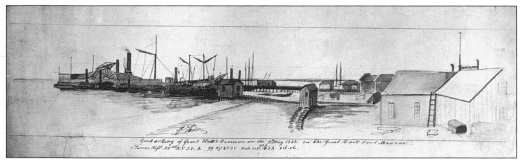

Lincoln was disappointed with the U.S. Navy's failure to reduce the Sewell's Point fortifications. The President viewed the entire action from Fort Wool's ramparts and quickly realized that Norfolk could not be captured by a naval attack. Therefore, Lincoln went out in a small boat and conducted his own reconnaissance of the coastline east of Willoughby's Spit. Lincoln, according to one Northern correspondent, "infused new vigor in both naval and military operations here" and selected Ocean View as the site for landing. Fort Wool continued to shell the Confederate batteries as the troops were readied on Fort Monroe for embarkation. Secretary Stanton noted that the "Sawyer gun at Fort Wool has silenced one battery on Sewell's Point. The James rifle mounted on Fort Wool also does good work . . . . The troops will be ready in an hour to move."

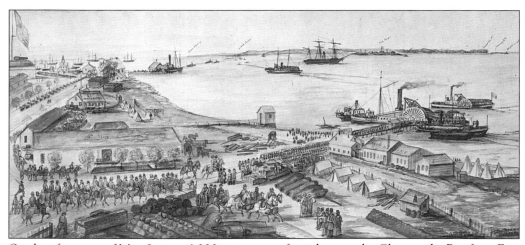

On the afternoon of May 9, over 6,000 troops were ferried across the Chesapeake Bay from Fort Monroe to Ocean View in canal boats. The first wave was commanded by Brigadier General Max Weber and the second was led by Brigadier General Joseph F. Mansfield. General Wool assumed command of the entire operation on the morning of May 10 and reached Norfolk by late afternoon. Norfolk, however, had already been abandoned by the Confederate troops commanded by Major General Benjamin Huger. Huger, fearing that his 10,000-man command would be cut off from retreat by the Union advance, set fire to Gosport Navy Yard, destroyed equipment that could not be moved, and marched his troops to Suffolk. Once Norfolk was occupied, the CSS *Virginia* was left without a base and the ironclad's new commander, Flag Officer Josiah Tattnall, was faced with a difficult decision.

Tattnall wanted to attack the Union fleet with his ironclad, destroying several enemy vessels before sinking in a blaze of glory. However, the need to help defend Richmond led to an effort to lighten the deep draft vessel so that it could steam up the James River. The reduction in draft proved to be futile. The *Virginia* was then run aground off Craney Island, and around 4:30 a.m. on the morning of May 11, the vessel was destroyed by her crew. S.R. Franklin observed the scene from his ship anchored off Fort Monroe writing that the ironclad's destruction "was a beautiful sight to us in more sense than one. She had been a thorn in our side for a long time, and we were glad to have her out of the way."

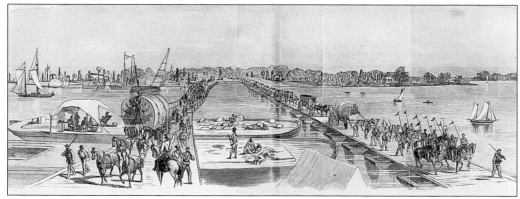

Once the *Virginia* was destroyed, the Federal fleet was able to move up the James River and support McClellan's operations outside the Confederate capital. Fort Monroe, however, was no longer required as the main supply base for the Union Army as it strove to capture Richmond. Nevertheless, Fort Monroe had served the Union well during the early stages of the Peninsula Campaign. The fort provided McClellan's army with protection from any excursion by the Confederate ironclad and had greatly supported the successful effort to expand Union control of Hampton Roads. Despite all his advantages, McClellan's campaign ended in failure at the gates of Richmond. The Army of the Potomac encamped for several weeks at Harrison's Landing 30 miles from the Confederate capital. President Lincoln, frustrated by McClellan's delays, decided to unite McClellan's troops with Major General John Pope's command outside of Washington. This engraving depicts the return of McClellan's army to Fort Monroe en route to Northern Virginia.

Seven

SOLDIER LIFE

For the soldiers who made up a portion of its garrison, life at Fort Monroe was very different from what many of their comrades were experiencing. To begin with, Fort Monroe was a large and secure base with adequate communication to the North by sea. Various supplies could be brought with little difficulty, and goods could be bought from the post sutler or the local stores. Living accommodation, though often crowded, was not nearly as crude as that in the field. Also, as the war's activities moved farther afield from the fort along the Peninsula or into the Carolinas, the fort became more stable in its daily routine. This photograph of the main gate, taken c. 1864, shows a rather relaxed atmosphere, which may have been produced by the fort's relative safety. While the military department headquartered there was still involved in many important events, and though some of the fort's units were sent out to fight in various campaigns, any threat to the fort had passed by the summer of 1862. Fort Monroe was able to develop its own style of life.

ENE IN ADAMS EXPRESS OFFICE, AT FORTRESS MONROE, VA., IN 1861—VOLUNTEERS RECEIVI

Mail has always been a constant source of pleasure for soldiers far from home. It was the same for those serving at Fort Monroe during the Civil War. The regularity of communication with the North meant that mail and packages could be sent and received with confidence. Many of the letters and diary entries of those serving at the fort record their desire to receive news from home or request articles and food to be sent to them. The soldiers also frequently sent part of their pay home to parents and wives. This print shows activities around the Adams Express Company offices at Fort Monroe. The proper receipt of packages was a concern, and an entry in the fort's daybook for Christmas 1864 notes that Captain Jerome Titlow, of the 3rd Pennsylvania Heavy Artillery, was given the task of ensuring that all packages were distributed appropriately.

The units making up the fort's garrison were frequently called upon to participate in most of the battles and campaigns taking place within the military department. There was also the daily round of soldierly activities to occupy the troops. There were daily formations and inspections, drills, guard mounts, and sentry duty. Of course, such a life could become boring from lack of diversity. As one soldier wrote to his wife in 1861, "Being in the same place there is nothing but the normal routine day in and day out. The officers and men have considerable leisure time and no man can complain of having too much to do." This 1864 photograph shows the 3rd Pennsylvania Heavy Artillery drawn up for an inspection on the post's parade ground. The days were filled with such events, but Sundays were generally given over to dress inspections and rest. The same soldier's letter described the church services at the Chapel of the Centurion, which was dedicated in 1858, "today attend[ed] church in the fort. The Episcopal service was used; the church is a modern one, Gothic style with an organ, aisle carpeted so that I felt as if I was at home again." However, a wife of a New England soldier noted that "We go in the Fort to church always, and it is surprising to me that here are so few to attend. It was full time to commence when we went in last Sunday and there were only perhaps thirty in all, when there are thousands so near, and no other services. There is very little notice taken of the Sabbath here. If I am to live here I hope to see a good many New England customs introduced, and one of the first should be an observance of the Sabbath Day." Certain holidays were observed, especially Christmas, and the soldiers were allowed a day off from all but "necessary" duties.

The officers had their round of duty to perform as well. In the photograph above, taken on the old post parade ground, the officer with the sword is the Officer of the Day. The sash across his shoulder indicates this status. On September 10, 1861, Captain Salmon Winchester of the 10th New York Infantry (on the right) wrote a letter to his cousin in which he described his daily round of duties. "In the morning, reveille beats at 5. The Drummers' Call beats at 4 1/2, at which time I have to get up to be ready to attend reveille. I have to be present, to see that the men all turn out and answer to their names. After reveille is over I return to my quarters and get ready for morning drill, which commences at 6. I then repair to the Parade Ground, to which the company is brought by the Orderly Sergeant, where I drill them till 7 1/2. I then go to my mess room and eat my breakfast and put on my full uniform for dress parade, which is at 8. Dress parade lasts about an hour. If I am not detailed as Officer of the Day, I can then go to my quarters. But when I am detailed for that duty, I go on the Parade Ground as soon as Parade is over, and receive and review the Guard. The Officer of the Day has the supervision of the entire Fort—a sort

of Captain of Police. He has sole charge of the guard, and of all the prisoners. He signs all the passes for soldiers to go outside the fort, is responsible for the cleanliness and regularity of the garrison, & c. During the night I have to visit every sentinel, to see that he is wide awake and understands his duty. I also have to visit the picket guard, who is stationed about three miles in the woods. But if I am not detailed for this duty, I can go to my quarters till 5 o'clock in the afternoon and the remainder of the time is devoted to company business, hearing complaints and dealing justice to refractory soldiers. At 5 o'clock is the Battalion drill where the Regimental line is formed and put through a variety of evolutions till 7, at which time comes Retreat Roll-Call. At 7 1/2 I go to tea and the labors of the day are ended."

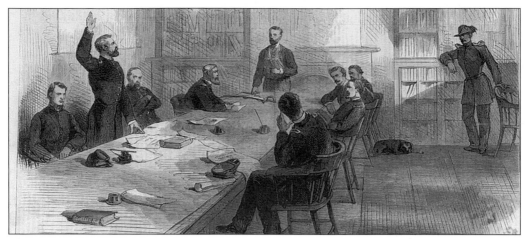

The mention of prisoners and refractory soldiers is a good reminder that in every organization there are those who will not abide by lawful discipline and authority. As the illustration shows and as the daybooks attest, courts-martial were not unusual. Common matters for their deliberation were drunkenness, failure to follow orders, and absence from duty. The second drawing illustrates the results of one of those courts-martial. It was traditional for thieves to be drummed out of the fort, while made to wear a sign naming their crime. For others, the punishment might be confinement in the fort's stockade. The stockade was located in the casemates just inside the main gate. It consisted of a large prison-room and a separate room containing individual cells. In an official report of 1870, it was described as follows: "The prison-rooms are badly ventilated. Both the windows and the embrasure are shielded by immovable blinds, which prevent the ingress of sunlight and interfere greatly with the wind, which otherwise would more freely enter the prison-room. The only ventilation to this room, which oftentimes has from twenty to forty men confined in it is furnished through the small embrasure. Into this prison-room sunlight scarcely ever enters, and never warms. During the winter the room is heated by stoves, which keep it comparatively dry and comfortably warm. In the summer time, however, it is always damp and the water condenses in large drops on the walls and trickles thence to the floor. The cells are much worse. They are contracted, ill ventilated, never warmed, and the light of the sun never reaches them. They are always cold, damp, most disagreeable, and really unfit to confine men in." It could not have been any better five years earlier.

The fort's relative safety and stability made it possible for the wives of several officers and of a few enlisted men to come and live at the fort. Although the atmosphere of the fort remained distinctly masculine, the presence of women made life a bit more civilized. The fort's housing and that of the surrounding areas were crowded with soldiers. However, accommodation for some married couples and even for some single officers was accomplished through the conversion of the old casemates. With the modernization of the fort's armament, the old 32-pounder seacoast guns in the casemates were no longer needed. The empty spaces were turned into quarters. The photograph above, dating to the Civil War, shows a couple and a guest inside a typical casemate living room. Furnishings had to be purchased or brought by the occupants themselves, leading one wife to complain, "We have sent to Boston for furniture enough to keep house here, and when that comes, will 'neither borrow nor lend.' Every thing is so very dear here, that I am determined that I will wait until my own things come."

The photograph above shows some of the officers of the 3rd Pennsylvania Heavy Artillery and their wives outside the casemate quarters of their commanding officer, Colonel Joseph Roberts. In addition to garrisoning the fort, the regiment's individual batteries participated in the siege of Suffolk, expeditions along the James, Chickahominy, and Nansemond Rivers, the siege of Petersburg, the expeditions against Fort Fisher, and Appomattox. On the "home front" at the fort, life was changeable. Verna Winchester, wife of Captain Salmon Winchester of the 10th New York Infantry, wrote the following to her cousin in October 1861: "Between you and me, Ella, if you want to go anywhere to enjoy yourself, don't think of visiting Fortress Monroe, for you are not allowed to wink here without a pass. No citizen allowed to walk upon the ramparts unattended by an officer of the garrison. Not allowed to walk upon the beach to pick up shells or watch the surf break upon the shore or go outside of your quarters without a pass from Gen. Wool." However, by the next month, things had improved and Verna Winchester was able to write to her cousin about being a guest at a supper and ball where she met a Swedish baron and a count. She then went on to write that the "greatest charm" of the fort "are its splendid sunsets. I do not think anywhere else upon this continent will you see such a lovely sight. For hours every night the skies are a moving panorama of pictures, continually changing, of sunshine and shadow, light and shade, and deeply dyed with every color of the rainbow. When the music of the *Minnesota*'s band comes in at your casement, mellowed by distance and you watch across the waters the fading of those lovely tints as twilight deepens then—imagine the rest Ella. I am not sentimental today and language fails me."

Not all the women who came to Fort Monroe were wives of officers. Some fortunate spouses of enlisted soldiers were also permitted to accompany their husbands to the post. The photograph to the right shows Sophia Saxton Leonard, the wife of Sergeant Loren Leonard, of the 3rd Pennsylvania Heavy Artillery. She was able to come to Fort Monroe in 1864. They originally had quarters in Hampton and later moved inside the fort. She helped to support the household by making pies, which she sold to soldiers. By this time the proscription noted by Mrs. Winchester must have been lifted, for it is known that Sophia Leonard walked along the beach for enjoyment, collecting shells that are still among the possessions of her family in Pennsylvania.

Loren Leonard was drafted into the Army on October 16, 1862. He was enrolled in Company D of the 3rd Pennsylvania Heavy Artillery and eventually rose to the rank of sergeant. He was fortunate in being allowed to have his wife obtain a position as a laundress. She was thus not only entitled to join her husband at Fort Monroe, but draw pay and rations. Sergeant Leonard was made sergeant of the Provost Guard (the badge for which he wears in this photograph) and was later promoted to second lieutenant.

The fort's geographic location was also responsible for one other important aspect of life there during the war. Being so close to several fronts in Virginia and the Carolinas, and with rapid communication by steamer from many battlefields, Fort Monroe was a natural location to place a major hospital. The picture above shows the post's original hospital as it looked in 1862, when a wounded Union officer painted a watercolor of it. While it was adequate enough for the peacetime garrison, it would soon be overwhelmed with the number of men who needed to be looked after.

Some of the earliest arrivals in the hastily sent militia regiments would be among the first patients of the hospital. Not all were there for treatment for wounds received in battle. The diseases of camp claimed victims among young men who had never before had to live in such close quarters with others. Poor sanitation in the field also caused illness. Diseases such as dysentery and diarrhea took many lives. The photograph to the left shows Private E.T. Collier of the 3rd Massachusetts who died of typhoid fever at the Hygeia hospital at Fort Monroe in 1861. He died before he ever heard a shot fired in anger.

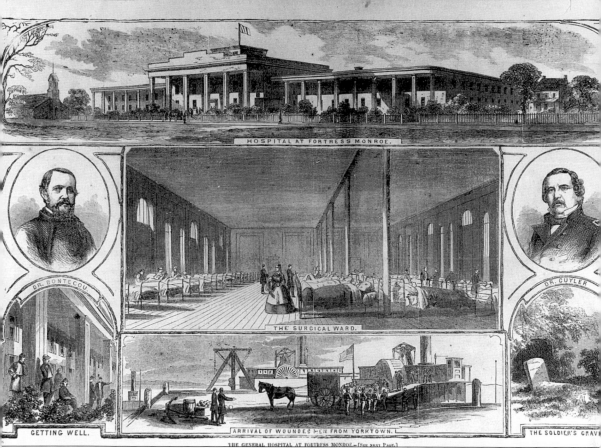

THE GENERAL HOSPITAL AT FORTRESS MONROE.—[See next Page.]

A quick solution for the lack of adequate accommodation for the sick and wounded was to take over a wing of the famous Hygeia Hotel. Its guestrooms and large communal areas provided space for wards and offices. Seven officers, plus several nurses, orderlies, and hospital doctors, for this growing establishment also had to increase. The print above shows what the Hygeia Hospital looked like by the late spring of 1862, along with portraits of its two head doctors, Surgeons Reed B. Bontecou and John M. Cuyler. Bontecou joined the 2nd New York Infantry as a surgeon in September 1861. At the war's end, he had been promoted by brevet to lieutenant colonel for his service. Cuyler was a "regular" who had joined the Army as an assistant surgeon in 1834. He was a major and a surgeon when the war began. In 1862, he was promoted to lieutenant colonel and was a medical inspector. For his "faithful and meritorious" service, he was brevetted to colonel and brigadier general. The Hygeia Hospital was a primary point of evacuation for wounded men from the Peninsula Campaign, which by the late spring of 1862 was nearing its climax in the battles outside Richmond. The hotel itself continued to accommodate crowds of curiosity seekers, newspaper correspondents, and other persons who had come to see the operations of the Army. These large numbers of civilians in the vicinity of the fort were an embarrassment to the command and a concern to the authorities in Washington. Therefore, in spite of its role as a hospital and infamous reputation, the entire Hygeia was torn down by order of the Secretary in 1862. A part of the Hygeia complex not connected with the main structure was left standing near the postern gate and was used for a time as a hospital until it too was demolished. The proprietor was given permission to open a one-story restaurant, called the Hygeia Dining Saloon in the vicinity of the wharf, for the benefit of the soldiers and civilian workers at the fort.

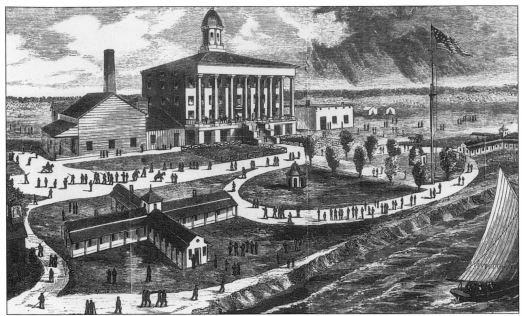

Again, some existing facilities were taken over. In nearby Hampton there was an imposing structure, located on the banks of Hampton Roads, which had been the Chesapeake Female Seminary. This school was taken over in November 1861 and converted to a hospital. Under its new name of the Chesapeake Hospital, it would exist throughout the war and beyond, treating wounded and sick officers. Captured Confederate soldiers also received the same treatment when they arrived here. In the print above, the central building was the old Seminary, which served as the main hospital. The two single-floor, X-shaped buildings were wards for patients, and these were joined by a circular path, which could be used for exercise.

This rare photograph shows the main building of the Chesapeake Hospital with some temporary quarters along its side. While it is difficult to determine from the photograph, these tents are very likely the quarters for the 150 men of the Veterans Reserve Corps, who performed police and guard duties at the hospital.

Another hospital was raised near the Chesapeake Hospital in 1862—the United States General Hospital, Hampton. This hospital for enlisted men was of a simpler design, but equally efficient in caring for the thousands of wounded who came through its wards in the course of the war. The Hampton Hospital was about a quarter mile from the Chesapeake Hospital and consisted of 30 single-floor cottages, formed in a triangle. This photograph shows the buildings of the Hampton Hospital and the Chesapeake Hospital in the background. In the far distance, ships of the Union Navy can be seen in Hampton Roads. In addition to the hospital wards, there were a kitchen, grounds, a pharmacy, a chapel, and quarters for doctors and staff. An 1864 article in *Harper's New Weekly Magazine* described the work at the hospitals as follows: "Sickness of every possible kind, and wounds of every conceivable variety, are to be treated in its wards. [The patients are] surrounded with a corps of conscientious, sympathizing, and accomplished practitioners. The most deadly wound, the most insidious disease, will, in these wards, find all that modern skill can furnish to give relief."

This print from *Frank Leslie's Illustrated Newspaper* dated 1862 shows the horse-drawn railroad that had been built at the fort during the war. This railroad helped bring supplies from the numerous steamers to the various quartermaster depots and storage yards that were established at the fort. During the battles and campaigns that took place in Virginia and North Carolina, the railroad also served another purpose. Special covered cars were brought to the wharf, and wounded soldiers from the ships were placed on them. The railroad then brought these men to the hospitals, offering a smoother ride than any ambulance.

There were several doctors and surgeons who served at the hospitals near Fort Monroe. Because of the large numbers of patients, especially after a major battle, the duty was long and arduous. One of these doctors was John Herr Frantz, shown in the carte-de-visite photograph above. He was appointed an assistant surgeon in the Army on May 28, 1861. His first service was with the 8th and 19th U.S. Infantry Regiments. He served on the Peninsula between February 27 and July 24, 1862, and was on an expedition up the York River. He was the chief medical purveyor at Fort Monroe from July 24, 1862, to December 1863. He then was in North Carolina as the acting medical purveyor at New Bern, a position he held until February 29, 1864. He returned to Virginia as the surgeon in charge of Balfour General Hospital, Portsmouth. He ended his Civil War service back at Fort Monroe as surgeon in charge of the General Hospital, where he served from July 22, 1865, until March 21, 1866. While there, he married a local woman, Louise Sewall, in the post chapel.

Another doctor was Ely McClellan. He was appointed an assistant surgeon on August 5, 1861. By 1864, he was a full surgeon and was in charge of the Hampton General Military Hospital and the Chesapeake Military Hospital. Seven officers, nurses, orderlies, and hospital stewards assisted him. The Hampton General Military Hospital opened its doors for patients in August 1862, just as General McClellan's army was returning to the Fort Monroe area. An article in *Harper's New Monthly Magazine*, dated November 1864, provides the following statistics for the hospital up to April 26, 1864: 6,540 patients were received and treated. Of that number, 4,491 were recovered and returned to duty; 1,049 were transferred to the Veterans Reserve Corps; 784 remained at the hospital; and 216 died.

Eight

Operations along the James and the Peninsula

When General Wool left Fort Monroe on June 2, 1862, he turned command of the Department of Virginia over to Major General John A. Dix. Like General Butler, General Dix was given a politically inspired commission by Abraham Lincoln at the start of the war. General Dix had a long and distinguished career in his native New York. He joined the Army in 1812 at the age of 14, serving as an ensign in the 10th U.S. Infantry. He remained in the Army for 16 years, rising to the rank of captain before he resigned his commission in 1828. He then followed a career in law and politics, becoming a Jacksonian Democrat and serving as a county administrator, adjutant general of the state, secretary of state, state school supervisor, and U.S. senator. He served as the secretary of the treasury at the very end of the Buchanan administration, at which time he told one of his agents in New Orleans that if anyone tried to lower the American flag, he was to "shoot him on the spot." For this display of spirit, his military experience, and his support as a Democrat, President Lincoln made John Dix a major general of volunteers, to date from May 16, 1861. Because of this early appointment, he was the senior volunteer general throughout the war. Within the year after taking command at Fort Monroe, the military department there would be renamed twice, but would ultimately retain its status as an independent command. During his tenure, the department also would be involved in some ancillary campaigns that were supportive of the operations of the Army of the Potomac.

In the early spring of 1863, the Federal IX Corps, under Major General Ambrose Burnside, was in Hampton Roads. The corps was soon ordered to Ohio under Major General John G. Parke. But it detached one of its divisions to reinforce the garrison at Suffolk. This presence caused the Confederate command to send reinforcements to the southside of the James to counter any moves against Richmond. At the same time, General Robert E. Lee's Army of Northern Virginia needed fresh supplies of food and fodder. Such stores were relatively untouched on the south side of the James River and southeastern Virginia. In April, General Lee sent a corps comprised of two divisions, under the command of Lieutenant General James Longstreet (left), to this region. General Longstreet saw an opportunity to gather supplies. An important outpost of the Union on the southside was the town of Suffolk. General Longstreet determined to recapture this town, reclaiming the area for the Confederacy and threatening Norfolk. For three and a half-weeks he laid siege to the town, beginning on April 11, 1863. The Union forces there were under the command of Major General John J. Peck (seen here), who was seriously wounded in the fighting. By May 4, 1863, unable to capture the town despite determined assaults on the Union positions, Longstreet returned to Northern Virginia. However, he had stayed away too long. During his absence, General Lee had fought his brilliant Chancellorsville campaign against major General Joseph Hooker. This was a great victory for Robert E. Lee; it might have been greater still had Longstreet and his corps been with him.

Another expedition soon followed. After the Battle of Chancellorsville, Robert E. Lee saw an opportunity to invade the North for a second time. Moving his army into Maryland and Pennsylvania, he not only posed a threat to those areas, but also to Washington itself. General Hooker, still in command of the Army of the Potomac through June, had to keep his army between Lee's army and the Capitol. The same instructions were given to Major General George G. Meade when he replaced General Hooker. As the armies formed for battle in Pennsylvania, the Union command in Washington ordered General Dix to launch an expedition along the Virginia Peninsula to threaten Richmond, and thus keep some reinforcements from being sent to General Lee's army. General Dix ordered the IV Corps, under Major General Erasmus D. Keyes, to make a demonstration against Richmond. Another column was led by Brigadier General George W. Getty to threaten rail communications and bridges leading to Lee's army from the north of Richmond. (Getty, at right, would be the commander of Fort Monroe from 1877 to 1883.) These feints made by General Dix had the desired effect.

Troops that could have gone to aid General Lee were held back by Richmond. One other result of the campaign was the capture of Robert E. Lee's son, Brigadier General William H.F. Lee. He was held as a hostage at Fort Monroe until Union officers imprisoned in Richmond received proper treatment.

General Dix turned over the command of the Department of Virginia and Fort Monroe on July 15, 1863. General Dix took command of the Department of the East and rendered valuable service in putting down the draft riots that had broken out in New York City. His successor was Major General John Gray Foster (pictured at left). At this time, the separate Departments of Virginia and of North Carolina were consolidated into a single Department of Virginia and North Carolina. This large department included the area of the Peninsula as far as Williamsburg to Yorktown and across the York River to Gloucester Point; the Eastern Shore of Virginia; Norfolk and Portsmouth and Newport News; and the area of North Carolina to include Beaufort, New Bern, Plymouth, and Washington. By November, the district had a total of about 32,500 troops.

Major General Benjamin Butler returned to Fort Monroe in November 1863. He was again the commanding general of the department, and would be in that position during the opening of the campaigns of 1864, the war's bloodiest year. To ensure that the troops in the Department of Virginia and North Carolina were in the best position to support the upcoming battles of the Army of the Potomac, a new army was created. The Army of the James, with General Butler as its commander, was formed on April 28, 1864. This new army drew its troops and units from those within the department, and even from South Carolina. They were formed into two corps: the X, commanded by Major General Quincy Adams Gilmore; and the XVIII, commanded by Major General William F. Smith. Ever since President Lincoln's Emancipation Proclamation, the Union Army had been actively recruiting African Americans into its ranks. Many of these units of United States Colored Troops were in the Army of the James, particularly in the XVIII Corps.

The Union armies had a new commanding general by the start of 1864. Lieutenant General Ulysses S. Grant came with a clear idea of what he wanted for the upcoming spring campaigns, a coordinated offensive by all the Union armies against the Confederacy. The primary focus was on the operations of the Army of the Potomac against the Confederate Army of Northern Virginia, but all forces would have a role to play. In early April, General Grant came to Fort Monroe and met with General Butler. For three days, he discussed with General Butler his plans for the Army of the James in the coming campaign. Their immediate objective was Petersburg, a key to Richmond itself and a center of communications and supply for Lee's army. General Grant also ordered General Butler to capture and hold onto City Point, located at the confluence of the James and Appomattox Rivers.

To hide the intentions of his army, General Butler had the Army of the James assemble at Yorktown and Gloucester Point. On May 4, 1864, the Army of the Potomac opened its Wilderness Campaign. That night, both corps of the Army of the James boarded transports that took them to Hampton Roads. There, they joined up with a Union fleet of ironclads and gunships. The following morning at 6:00, General Butler led the large procession on its way from the steamer *Greyhound*. He was seen on the deck waving his hat forward, as if to encourage men and ships to their tasks. The 30,000-man army landed that same day in the vicinity of City Point and Bermuda Hundred. The chance for a great victory was in reach. But General Butler vacillated too long, not attacking the Confederate lines defending the way to Richmond until May 13. This delay gave the Confederates time to react. Reinforcements from the Carolinas were sent to General P.G.T. Beauregard, who used them to drive the Union Army back into its lines at Bermuda Hundred. There he kept them bottled up, unable to provide any more assistance to their brethren fighting in Northern Virginia even as the Confederates were able to reinforce Lee's army. The missed opportunity led to General Grant eventually shifting his army across the James River and linking up with General Butler. City Point, still held by the Union Army in accordance with General Grant's original instructions, would become the great port and logistics base for the Petersburg Campaign.

The Army of the James would continue to play an active part in Petersburg for the next several months. Since this was the first time that so many units of United States Colored Troops were engaged in combat, their actions and performance were observed with interest. Because of the large population of contrabands which had settled around the fort, two regiments of United States Colored Cavalry and Battery B, 2nd United States Colored Light Artillery were recruited there. The print above shows this battery in action, firing on Confederate positions during the Petersburg Campaign. This battery would later serve at Richmond and Portsmouth. In 1866, the battery was sent to the Rio Grande, where it was part of the United States' show of force on the Mexican border.

There were 25 regiments of United States Colored Troops in the Army of the James. They served in such engagements as New Market Heights and Darbytown Road. The painting above shows a charge of the 22nd United States Colored Infantry at Petersburg in June 1864. This regiment served in both the X and XVIII Corps. General Butler had a special interest and pride in the performance of the African-American troops under his command. He ensured that their bravery was rewarded where appropriate. Sixteen of these soldiers and four of their officers received the Congressional Medal of Honor for their actions in this campaign. General Butler also had a special Army of the James medal struck and issued to soldiers of his command who had distinguished themselves in battle.

By late 1864, General Butler was again at Fort Monroe, where he was still the commanding general of the Department of the Army of Virginia and North Carolina. His mission now was to capture Fort Fisher at Cape Fear, North Carolina. The strong fortifications there guarded the entrance to Wilmington, the last major port the Confederacy held on the east coast. A railroad line ran directly from Wilmington to General Lee's army at Petersburg. This city was therefore of vital importance to the Confederacy; its capture would hasten the fall of Petersburg and Richmond and be a major step to ending the war. By December 8, 1864, General Butler had assembled a force of 6,500 men, mostly from the Army of the James, at Fort Monroe. There, they boarded transports and sailed south to join the Navy fleet under Admiral David Dixon Porter.

General Butler's plan was to run a ship filled with powder against the walls of the fort. The resultant explosion would level the walls and make the way easier for the infantry. Accordingly, an old gunship, the *Louisiana*, was chosen and packed with 215 tons of black powder. On the night of December 23, she was run aground 250 yards off the fort. While the powder did go off, and the *Louisiana* was entirely destroyed, there was no damage to the fort.

Admiral Porter had command of the largest fleet of U.S. warships ever assembled: a total of 57 warships mounting 627 heavy caliber guns. With the failure of the powder boat scheme, he poured an intense barrage into the fort the next day, and a landing was made on December 25. However, the 2,000 soldiers who had been put ashore found that the fort was still too strong to be taken. After a few hours they were taken off the beach and returned to the ships. General Butler returned to Hampton Roads, while Admiral Porter wrote to the authorities in Washington about the necessity to try again. The failure was General Butler's last. He was relieved of command on January 8, 1865.

General Butler's place was taken by Major General Alfred H. Terry. General Terry had served with the Union Army since First Bull Run. He had proven his worth in South Carolina in the Port Royal campaign, the reduction of Fort Pulaski, and also at the siege of Fort Wagner. He was a division commander in the Army of the James during the Petersburg Campaign. For the second Fort Fisher campaign, he was given the same troops with an additional reinforcement of 1,500 men. Once again, transports assembled off Fort Monroe. The Army portion of the expedition rendezvoused with the Navy fleet on January 12.

Admiral Porter made certain that the Navy's bombardment was more effective this time. Emphasizing deliberate firing at the fort's guns and the knocking down of the earthen parapets and traverses, the fleet's guns opened fire in the early morning of January 13. Once again, all 627 guns played a part, but this time the bombardment lasted for two days. A total of 19,682 well-aimed rounds were fired at the defenders. Admiral Porter would later report that "Traverses began to disappear and the southern angle of Fort Fisher commenced to look very dilapidated."

General Terry's force started to land just four hours after the commencement of the bombardment. By 3:00 p.m., all 8,000 were ashore, 2 miles from the Confederate fort. The final assault was planned for the morning of January 15, by which time only one Confederate gun was capable of firing. Early the next morning at 3:00 a.m., the fleet's guns suddenly fell silent, and all of its steam whistles screamed in unison. This was the signal for the charge. The Union forces came in two columns. One half of General Terry's men held an entrenchment guarding against possible Confederate reinforcements, while the other 4,000 attacked down the landward side of the fort. At the same time a force of 2,000 sailors and Marines advanced along the beach. The fighting was terrible and at close quarters. Colonel William Lamb, Fort Fisher's commander, later stated, "If there has ever been a longer or more stubborn hand-to-hand encounter, I have failed to meet with it in history." The Confederate resistance at last gave way. The fort surrendered at 10:00 that night. With its loss, Union forces soon occupied Wilmington, and the last link of the Confederacy to the outside world was closed.

By late January 1865, the ever-tightening noose around the Confederacy caused some members of its government to reach out for any accommodation that might bring peace. Although the idea of Confederate independence was a stumbling block for both sides in any negotiations, President Lincoln decided to make the effort when Confederate authorities proposed a commission be formed to pursue the subject of peace. He traveled to Hampton Roads aboard the *River Queen*, anchoring just off Fort Monroe and the protection of its guns. He and Secretary of State William H. Seward met with Confederate Vice President Alexander Stephens, Robert M.T. Hunter (the presiding officer of the Confederate Senate), and Confederate Assistant Secretary of War John Campbell. They talked for four hours. But in the end the war would go on. The Confederate insistence on independence, and the Union insistence that the seceded states lay down their arms and return to the Union were irreconcilable. Just two months later, Washington would receive a telegram relayed through the telegrapher at Fort Monroe, "We took Richmond at 8.15 this morning."

With the war winding down on all fronts, there was still much activity centering on Fort Monroe. The large population of "contrabands," who had settled near "the Freedom Fort," would need special care and assistance. As a part of this aid, a separate hospital had been built for their treatment at Fort Monroe. In March, Harriet Tubman, the great heroine of the Underground Railroad, was appointed as the matron, or chief nurse, at this hospital. She remained at work there until July. She then returned to her home in Auburn, New York. She lived out the remainder of her life there, taking care of her elderly parents and anyone else who needed help. Her efforts to receive a pension or other renumeration for her work with the Union Army were unsuccessful. She did finally receive a pension as the widow of her second husband, Nelson Davis, who had served in the Army of the James in the 8th U.S. Colored Infantry.

Samuel Chapman Armstrong was born in the Kingdom of Hawaii to missionary parents. While completing his college education in New York, he had joined the Union Army as a captain. By 1864, he was a colonel commanding the 8th regiment of United States Colored Infantry, serving with it throughout the Petersburg Campaign. He was brevetted brigadier general effective March 13, 1865. Shortly after, he accepted the position of heading the local headquarters of the Bureau for Refugees, Freedmen, and Abandoned Lands, or the "Freedmen's Bureau."

The bureau had its offices at Fort Monroe in this small building. However, it would have large effects on the surrounding area. The purpose of the bureau was to bring some relief to the lot of the newly freed slaves and others set adrift by the upheavals of the war. General Armstrong described his work with the Freedmen's Bureau in June 1866 in a letter to his mother, "we issue 18,000 rations to those who would die of starvation were it not for this, and keep their children at school, and get them work and prevent injustice."

Although far removed from Washington, D.C., the fort had one small connection to the assassination of President Lincoln. Samuel Arnold was one of the original conspirators when the plan was only to kidnap the President. When the attempt failed in March 1865, he had left John Wilkes Booth's band. He came to Fort Monroe, where he apparently knew the sutler, John Wharton, and obtained a position with him. On April 17, just three days after the assassination, Arnold was arrested at Fort Monroe, along with Wharton and some of his other employees. While the others were quickly released, Samuel Arnold was brought to trial. Since he was not involved in the assassination, Arnold was not executed. He was sentenced to imprisonment in Fort Jefferson on the Dry Tortugas off the Florida coast. He was pardoned in 1869.

Nine

DAVIS IN CHAINS

With the breaking of the Confederate lines at Petersburg and the imminent fall of Richmond, Confederate President Jefferson Davis attempted to move his government west. He hoped to join up with one of the Confederate armies that was still operating, and thus prolong the war and the Confederacy. He was to be disappointed in this plan. The 4th Michigan Cavalry captured him on May 10, 1865, near Irwinville, Georgia. Immediately upon his capture, he was taken to Macon and then to Savannah. From that point he was brought to Hilton Head, South Carolina, and placed aboard the steamer *William P. Clyde*. The *Clyde* reached Fort Monroe on May 19, where one of the casemates had been prepared as a cell to hold him. Assistant Secretary of War Charles A. Dana and Major General Henry W. Halleck arrived at the fort on the 20th to oversee the preparations for Davis's imprisonment. On the 21st, Davis was separated from his family and the other prisoners, except for Confederate Congressman Clement C. Clay. Davis was eventually charged with three crimes: treason against the United States, maltreatment of Union prisoners of war, and complicity in the assassination of President Abraham Lincoln.

A new Military District of Fort Monroe was created on May 21. The new commanding general was Major General Nelson A. Miles. A 25-year-old officer noted for his bravery and ambition, he would receive the Medal of Honor for his actions at Chancellorsville and later rise to become the commanding general of the Army during the Spanish-American War. He was specially selected to take command of Fort Monroe during Davis's imprisonment. He arrived by a special steamer on the 22nd. Early in the afternoon of that day, a double line of soldiers was drawn up from the post's engineer wharf, leading through the East Gate and to the first front. General Miles personally escorted Davis behind a detachment of the 4th Michigan Cavalry. Davis and Clay were led to their cells, in casemates two and four respectively. Neither of them would set foot outside of these confines for several months.

Clement C. Clay, Jefferson Davis's partner in imprisonment, had been captured with him in Georgia. Clay had served as a Confederate congressman and was later the Confederate agent to Canada. Clay was placed in a cell similar to that of Jefferson Davis, which had been constructed in casemate four. The intervening casemate, number three, served two purposes. First, it held additional guards for the prisoners; second, the space between them kept the prisoners from communicating. Clay was sent a prayer book by his wife, which he kept during the period of his internment. He was finally released on parole in April 1866.

Strict precautions were taken to ensure that Davis could neither escape nor be rescued. As was written in the *New York Herald*, "Davis can never escape. Neither the great Napoleon at Elba or St. Helena, nor the lesser Napoleon at the Fortress of Ham was subjected to a greater surveillance. The great Corsican escaped from Elba, Napoleon the lesser escaped from Ham, but no such hope for Davis. He can never escape." The initial conditions of Davis's imprisonment were harsh, in many ways like solitary confinement. While two guards were in his cell at all times, they were not allowed to speak with him nor answer his questions. A light was kept burning day and night, and the slats of his cot were covered with a thin mattress and uncomfortable pillow. His diet was not the best, and a lack of appetite kept him from consuming what was offered. The close confinement, the constant light, the lack of rest occasioned by the continuous tread of the sentries in the room, the strain on his eyes from the glare of the whitewashed walls, and the small print of the Bible he was allowed to read all quickly conspired to break Davis's health.

Assistant Secretary Dana had written a deliberately vague instruction to the commanding general that he was "hereby authorized and directed to place manacles and fetters upon the hands and feet of Jefferson Davis and Clement C. Clay, whenever he may deem it advisable in order to render their imprisonment more secure." On the evening of the 23rd, the fort's blacksmith, Henry Arnold (pictured above), entered Davis's cell, accompanied by Captain Jerome Titlow of the 3rd Pennsylvania Heavy Artillery. Both Arnold and Titlow were there to execute Dana's orders and place Davis in irons. As he saw the shackles in the hands of the smith, Davis knew what was coming. Captain Titlow told Davis that he was responding to orders. As Arnold knelt to place the shackles about Davis's leg, the prisoner roused himself and struck the smith down. Arnold raised himself back up, holding his hammer in a threatening manner. Captain Titlow quickly threw himself between the two men and called for four unarmed guards to come in and hold Davis down on his cot until Arnold could complete his work. The next day, General Miles stated in his official report, "Yesterday I directed that irons be put on Davis's ankles, which he violently resisted, but became more quiet afterward." In his account of the incident, written years afterward, Captain Titlow recalled that "Just as I was going out Davis raised from his cot and threw his feet to the floor, and with the clanking of the chains he gave way. I will say here that it was anything but a pleasant sight to see a man like Jefferson Davis shedding tears."

The 24th of May was to prove an important day for Jefferson Davis during his captivity at Fort Monroe. On that day he received his first visit from Lieutenant Colonel John Craven, a United States Army surgeon and chief medical officer of the fort. Dr. Craven had a distinguished career during the war, having served as a medical officer in several expeditions, to include the capture of Port Royal, the siege of Fort Pulaski, and operations against Charleston in 1863. The picture above shows him operating in the field in South Carolina. In 1864, he was the chief medical officer for the X Corps in Virginia, and by 1865 he was the chief medical officer for the Department of Virginia and North Carolina. Thus, he was assigned as Jefferson Davis's medical attendant.

When Dr. Craven first entered Jefferson Davis's cell on May 24, he found him "very miserable and afflict[ed]" and wearing the shackles. "Stretched upon his pallet, and very much emaciated, Mr. Davis appeared a mere fascine of raw and tremulous nerves." A humanitarian spirit appears to have motivated Dr. Craven from this first meeting. He immediately began to do his best to alleviate some of the discomforts and other complaints, which were affecting his patient's health. One of the first things Dr. Craven was able to secure was permission for Davis to have tobacco for his pipe, one of the very few personal possessions he was allowed to keep. Dr. Craven also began to persuade General Miles to remove the shackles from the prisoner. In this the doctor was assisted by public opinion. When news became public of the rough handling Davis had received and of his being placed in irons, a great indignation was raised against such treatment. On the 28th, Secretary of War Edwin Stanton telegraphed General Miles to remove the shackles.

Another political prisoner arrived on June 17, 1865. This was John Mitchel, a staunch Irish nationalist. Mitchel had advocated armed resistance to British rule in Ireland, for which he was tried for treason and deported to Tasmania in 1848. In 1853, he escaped to the United States, where he worked as a journalist. During the war, he was editor-in-chief for the *Richmond Enquirer* and an associate editor for the *Richmond Examiner*. Mitchel had been a strong and uncompromising supporter of the Confederate cause. After his arrest in New York City, he was brought to Fort Monroe and placed in a cell in casement six. He remained there until October 19 when he was moved to other quarters on post. He was finally released at the end of that month. His imprisonment at Fort Monroe led him to be described as a "martyr to the effectiveness of the printed word." He eventually returned to his native Ireland, where he was elected to Parliament in 1875, but he was not allowed to take his seat.

The 3rd Pennsylvania Heavy Artillery had formed the main garrison of the fort since it was ordered to Fort Monroe. As the war ended, this large regiment was not immediately mustered out of the service. Instead, it had one last role to play. Its soldiers would form the greatest number of guards for Jefferson Davis and the other prisoners. Loren Leonard, shown in the photograph above, had been a sergeant in the regiment and was the sergeant of the Provost Guard for the post. He was promoted to second lieutenant on September 8, 1865, and continued to serve with the regiment until it was finally mustered out in November 1865. Lieutenant Leonard was a humane and thoughtful guard. He received a signed card from Clement C. Clay thanking him for his "kindness in distress in prison."

Dr. Craven worked unceasingly to improve the conditions of Jefferson Davis's imprisonment. He saw that Davis's diet was improved and that he be allowed to take an hour's exercise each day by walking on the ramparts of the fort. The first of these walks was on July 24, and was short due to Davis's weak condition. The continuous marching of the sentries in his cell was finally ended. Despite these improvements, Davis's health continued to deteriorate. Dr. Craven noticed that while he could often engage his patient in interesting conversation, he was increasingly despondent and weak and his eyesight was failing. Beginning in August, Dr. Craven began to push for a change of quarters as a means of improving Davis's mental interest and physical health. Receiving General Miles's support, permission was received to move Davis to a set of quarters prepared in Carroll Hall, an officer's barracks. Jefferson Davis moved into his new room on October 2. There, Davis's situation greatly improved. His quarters were larger, airier, and furnished with a fireplace and other furniture and a mosquito bar for his bed was provided. He was allowed to correspond, although with censorship, with friends and family. His wife was allowed to visit him on a few occasions. He was allowed to continue to take his daily exercise by walking the ramparts at night. Under these and other measures, Davis's health improved. In November, Dr. Craven apparently went too far in seeking to aid Jefferson Davis. Dr. Craven procured an overcoat and suitable clothing for the winter months for Davis. He was instructed to keep his conversation with the prisoner strictly to matters relating to his health. In December, Dr. Craven was relieved of attending to Davis. In January, he was mustered out of the service and went on to a successful career as a doctor and inventor. He also wrote a book relating his experiences with Davis entitled *The Prison Life of Jefferson Davis*.

TREASON MUST BE MADE ODIOUS.

As shown by this contemporary cartoon by Thomas Nast, entitled "Treason Must Be Made Odious," not everyone was pleased with the improved treatment that Jefferson Davis received. During 1866, Davis continued as a prisoner at Fort Monroe. In April of that year, Clement Clay was finally released, but Davis continued to await indictment and trial. The conspiracy charge was eventually dropped when it became obvious that it was based on forged evidence. After several false starts, Jefferson Davis was indicted for treason on May 10, 1866, in the Circuit Court of the United States for the District of Virginia. Davis was brought to Richmond on May 13, 1867, but the Attorney General objected to the trial at that term of the court. A motion to allow the accused to post bail was made and carried. Such prominent persons as Horace Greeley, Cornelius Vanderbilt, and Gerrit Smith signed a bail bond of $100,000. Jefferson Davis was finally discharged. The final trial was set to begin on December 3, 1868. By February 1869, the argument was made that President Johnson's general amnesty of the preceding year covered Jefferson Davis's case as well, and the indictments for treason were dismissed. Davis then traveled for a time in Europe. He returned to the United States with his family in 1870. He lived for a time in Memphis, Tennessee, working as the president of an insurance company. By 1877, he returned to Mississippi, settling on a plantation named Beauvoir, near Biloxi. Here he wrote his history of the Confederacy and lived out the remainder of his life. He died on December 6, 1889. In 1893, his body was reinterred in Hollywood Cemetery in Richmond, the resting place of many heroes of the Confederacy.

Ten

REMNANTS AND REMINDERS

Just as the war had a profound effect on American society, so did it change the lives of individuals who would serve at Fort Monroe and alter the communities surrounding it. This often-copied photograph shows Captain John C. Tidball (second from the left) and some of the officers of his battery during the war. Tidball served as an artillery officer in nearly every battle fought by the Army of the Potomac and rose to the rank of major general of volunteers by brevet. In 1880, while serving at Fort Monroe as superintendent for artillery instruction at the Artillery School, he wrote a detailed manual on the operations of heavy artillery. From 1883 to 1888, he ended a distinguished career by serving as the commanding general of Fort Monroe and as the commandant of the Artillery School.

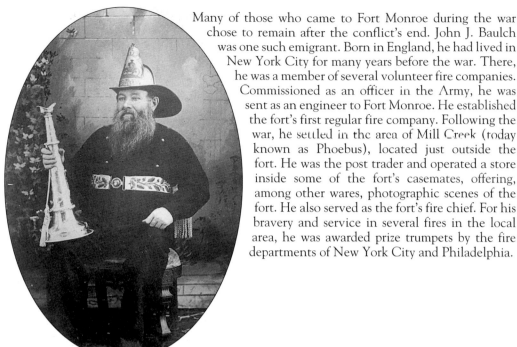

Many of those who came to Fort Monroe during the war chose to remain after the conflict's end. John J. Baulch was one such emigrant. Born in England, he had lived in New York City for many years before the war. There, he was a member of several volunteer fire companies. Commissioned as an officer in the Army, he was sent as an engineer to Fort Monroe. He established the fort's first regular fire company. Following the war, he settled in the area of Mill Creek (today known as Phoebus), located just outside the fort. He was the post trader and operated a store inside some of the fort's casemates, offering, among other wares, photographic scenes of the fort. He also served as the fort's fire chief. For his bravery and service in several fires in the local area, he was awarded prize trumpets by the fire departments of New York City and Philadelphia.

Another soldier who stayed on in the local area was Captain Jerome Titlow of the 3rd Pennsylvania Heavy Artillery. Captain Titlow had been the Officer of the Day when shackles were placed on Jefferson Davis. After the war he lived in Hampton, working in the lumberyard established by a fellow Pennsylvanian, Jacob Heffelfinger. Later, he became the sheriff of Elizabeth City County, the present-day city of Hampton. He served in that position for 11 years. He then moved west, living in the Dakotas and then St. Paul, where he spent the rest of his life. He eventually wrote at least three accounts of the shackling of Jefferson Davis and his part in it. His purpose was to keep the historical record straight, and he received the thanks of Mrs. Jefferson Davis, who used one of his accounts in her biography of her husband.

Major Franz von Schilling was another officer from the 3rd Pennsylvania Heavy Artillery. Von Schilling was born in Constatt, Germany, and had served in the Army of the Grand Duchy of Baden. He received permission to come to the United States in 1861. He joined the U.S. Army, rising to the rank of major and serving in Delaware and Virginia. After his discharge, he remained in the local area. He married Martha Booker, the daughter of a local planter, and became a farmer for several years. In the 1870s, he accepted an appointment with the U.S. Army engineers in Washington, D.C. He returned to his native Germany just prior to his death in 1895. Many of his descendants still reside in the area of Hampton.

Corporal Frank Larrabee served in the 14th Maine Infantry and was wounded at Port Hudson, Louisiana. After his discharge, he obtained an appointment as a clerk in the commissary department at Fort Monroe. Larrabee soon showed sound business sense, opening the Monitor Photographic Gallery at Fort Monroe, where he took some of the pictures in this book. After the war, he continued to live in the area of Hampton, establishing a pharmacy. He was appointed as a local magistrate for Elizabeth City County in 1869 and continued to hold that post until the 1890s. He was a member of the Public School Board and was the Master of the Monitor Masonic Lodge at Fort Monroe. Larrabee Street in Phoebus is named for him.

VIEW OF THE U.S. HOSPITALS, BET

After the war, the need for the large hospital facilities quickly disappeared. Most of the temporary wooden buildings of the Hampton General Military Hospital were torn down, but the Chesapeake Military Hospital remained. It was bought by Benjamin F. Butler, who then sold it to the government for use as the Southern Branch of the National Home for Disabled Volunteer Soldiers. The home opened in 1870 and continued to provide care for Union veterans

EN. FORTRESS MONROE & HAMPTON, VA

until 1946, when the last local veteran, Private Charles Woodcock of New York, died. The old hospital building was finally torn down early in the twentieth century. Today, this institution is known as the Hampton Veterans' Administration Center and Hospital, and it still provides medical care to the nation's veterans.

Many of the thousands of freedmen and their families who came to the fort remained in its environs after the war, living originally in the contraband camp established at Hampton. The area was often called "slabtown" because of its unfinished building materials. These men and women helped to establish the town of Phoebus and rebuild Hampton. Many of them became small farmers and fishermen, selling produce to the commissary or the hotels. Others obtained employment on or around the fort. Some gained prominence in the local community. William R. Davis had escaped from slavery in 1862, later lectured with the American Missionary Association, and was appointed as the keeper of the Old Point Comfort Light. Another man who escaped from bondage was Robert M. Smith, who attended classes in one of the refugee camps in Hampton and later became a blacksmith and merchant. He served as a member of the Hampton City Council and was the collector of customs at Old Point Comfort. Perhaps the most famous African American at Fort Monroe after the war was Booker T. Washington, who worked at the Hygeia Hotel while attending the Hampton Normal and Agricultural School. The descendants of many of these freedmen are still living in Hampton and Phoebus.

General Armstrong recognized that the freedmen around Fort Monroe needed more than the necessities of life. He also thought that they would benefit as new citizens through a proper education. In cooperation with the American Missionary Association, he helped to found the Hampton Normal and Agricultural School in 1868. The mission of the school was to prepare teachers and provide training in practical skills and trades. General Armstrong was the school's first principal, a position he held until his death in 1893.

Brevet Major General Emory Upton had gained well-deserved fame during the Civil War. Graduating in the Military Academy Class of 1861, he was brevetted a major general of volunteers in 1864. Recognized for his personal bravery and ability, he successfully commanded units of all three branches: artillery, infantry, and cavalry. With the war's end, he spent much of the remainder of his short life training soldiers and seeking to improve the Army. In 1877, he was assigned to Fort Monroe, where he was the superintendent of theoretical instruction at the Artillery School. While there, he published his book *The Armies of Europe and Asia*. He also began work on *The Military Policy of the United States*, which was published posthumously. This highly influential work contained this brilliant officer's thoughts on the reorganization of the Army, much of which were incorporated in the reforms of the administration of President Theodore Roosevelt.

The Army reestablished the Artillery School in 1867. Its first commander was Brevet Major General William F. Barry. General Barry had served in several campaigns in both the Eastern and Western theaters, and had a distinguished career as an artillerist. During his command, the school established a one-year course for new lieutenants, which included instruction in all types of artillery, gunnery and mathematics, the applications of artillery during campaigns and sieges, military law, and military history. The first class graduated in 1869. By 1871, one half of the artillery lieutenants had gone through the course. Throughout the rest of the century, the Artillery School was a model of military instruction and practice.

During the war, the fort received guns that were very modern and powerful by the standards of their day. However, with the war's end and the rapid reduction in forces and funding, the fort's armament was soon obsolete. Rodman guns, like those seen in the water battery, remained the main armament of the fort, even as other nations were adopting stronger, breech-loading guns of superior design and power.

As this photograph from the 1880s shows, the old muzzle-loading artillery was still placed about the fort decades after the war's end. In 1886, a board created by Secretary of War William C. Endicott recommended that the coastal defenses of the United States be modernized. The board called for separate batteries mounting new breech-loading guns to take the place of the old fortifications. However, due to the lack of sufficient funding, these recommendations were slow in being implemented. Some few new guns were mounted during the 1890s, but it was not until the Spanish-American War of 1898 that the modernization of Fort Monroe and other coastal defenses was rapidly brought up to date.

Other things were slow to change at Fort Monroe as well. This photograph from about 1890 shows a guard mount taking place just inside the Main Sally Port. The guardhouse and stockade were here, as they had been since the fort's original construction. Although there had been several uniform changes in the 1870s and 1880s, the uniforms worn by the soldiers still bear a strong resemblance to those worn by their Civil War predecessors. The Artillery School and the defenses of the Chesapeake Bay and Hampton Roads were not interrupted by any dramatic events until 1898 and the war with Spain.

The landscape of the fort did not change during this time. This photograph, taken from the ramparts and looking over the bridge leading to the Main Sally Port, shows the few buildings in that area until the turn of the century. The church in the background is Saint Mary Star of the Sea, a Roman Catholic church built in 1860. The small building just to the left of the road is standing on the area of the old Hygeia Hotel, torn down in 1862 and later rebuilt elsewhere.

The old casemates continued to be used for living quarters. The earlier photograph showing the couple in their quarters during the Civil War does not differ very much from this one taken in 1881, except for the design of the furniture. The carpets, besides being decorative, were necessary for keeping out dampness; so was the fireplace, which often contained a fire throughout the year to limit the growth of mold. The curtains over the archways hid the closets. There were no cooking facilities; meals could be taken at the local hotels. There weren't any bathrooms for these quarters. The closest latrine was about a block away. Eventually, Jefferson Davis's cell would be converted into a shower room.

Of course, some quarters were more spacious and comfortable than others, especially for senior officers. This photograph shows the widow of Brevet Brigadier General Rene DeRussy, the famous engineer officer, sometime in the late 1880s. Mrs. DeRussy is the lady wearing the shawl in the center, and she is shown with her daughters, son-in-law, grandchildren, and two servants. General DeRussy had died in 1865, and Mrs. DeRussy was actually no longer entitled to government quarters. However, no one had the heart to move her out. So there she stayed, in what came to be known as the DeRussy House, until she moved to New York City in 1891.

The most elegant quarters belonged to the commanding general. This photograph, taken in the late 1880s, shows the family of Brevet Major General John C. Tidball, who was then the commanding general and the commandant of the Artillery School. The stack of cannonballs to the right illustrates how the implements of the late war were still scattered about the post, and are still often found today in excavations. The gazebo was a nice feature of the backyard of the general's quarters. When the new set of commanding general's quarters was built in 1907, the gazebo was moved to the backyard of that building. There it remains, with some modifications and necessary repairs.

The post hospital was still located within the walls of the old fort. It was a three-story building, as seen in the left of this photograph from the 1880s. It contained a dispensary, storerooms, and four wards, which could accommodate ten beds. Behind the hospital were a detached kitchen and mess room. The hospital would continue to serve the needs of the post until the demands of the sick and wounded returning from the Spanish-American War overwhelmed it. It would be replaced by a larger, modern structure in 1899.

Even in times of economic hardship, necessary changes and improvements can be made. The enlisted men's quarters, which housed troops throughout the war, were in very poor condition. In a report dated 1870, the barracks were described as being too difficult to heat in the winter and too hot in summer. Great cracks had appeared in the joints, and in all, the quarters were uncomfortable for the men. Beds were still covered with straw that was changed every two days. By 1879, a new two-story barracks was built of brick, located on the north side of the parade ground.

There were, of course, diversions at the fort. The officers had separate quarters in Carroll Hall, where a mess was established as early as 1852. The Old Point Billiard Club began in 1869, but the club's building burned down on Christmas Eve, 1870. The mess and the club joined together in 1871 and moved into quarters in the casemates beneath the flagstaff bastion. The Fort Monroe Club became one of the fort's greatest institutions for nearly a century. Because of its location, an officer had to go inside the old fort to gain access. By 1894, a porch was built around the club along the moat. A small barge, christened the *Maid of the Moat*, was then installed to provide transportation across the water and easy access from the outside.

The club was soon celebrated for its congenial atmosphere. Here was a place where the officers could relax after their day's work with a game of billiards or just friendly conversation. When the noted military artist Robert F. Zogbaum arrived at Fort Monroe in 1893 on one of his visits, the club still maintained its distinctly masculine atmosphere, as shown in this painting. Women were not admitted until World War I.

A resort atmosphere also returned to Old Point Comfort during the post-war era. The original Hygeia Hotel was demolished in 1862 by order of the secretary of war. Secretary Stanton advised General Wool that the Hygeia was home to "a large number of visitors for pleasure, dealers in trade, and other persons not in the public service are now congregating at Fort Monroe, whose presence may embarrass the grave naval and military operations now in progress or in contemplation there. You are authorized, in your discretion, to require the immediate departure of all persons not in the service of the United States, whose presence may incommode operations and to exclude unauthorized persons from stopping or remaining there, until further notice. You will, from and after this date, exercise the most rigid discipline and police within the territory under your command." Caleb C. Williard, one of the hotel's owners, was granted permission in 1863 to build a one-story restaurant near the Baltimore Wharf. The eating establishment was

called the Hygeia Dining Saloon and was eventually purchased by Henry Clark. Clark applied to the War Department and on June 28, 1868, received approval to "enlarge the said hotel." The hotel ran into financial trouble in 1873, and it was acquired by Samuel M. Shoemaker in 1874. Shoemaker expanded the Hygeia and then sold it to local businessman Harrison Phoebus. Phoebus, who had originally moved to Old Point Comfort in 1866 as an agent for the Adams Express Company, immediately transformed the Hygeia into one of the finest hotels in the nation. The Hygeia was a huge, palatial structure, which could accommodate 1,000 guests. One observer noted that "Every room of this big wooden labyrinth has its drowsing occupant, and sleeping or waking, there are more beauties in the corridors of Hygeia or the shaded walks within the fort than one can meet in a decade of travel . . . Perhaps the proximity of Fortress Monroe has not a little to do with the popularity of Old Point Comfort as a health resort."

Phoebus continued to enlarge the hotel. *Harper's Weekly* reported in 1888 that the Hygeia was "substantially built, lusciously furnished with many of the rooms in suite and fitted with all the modern improvements . . . The wide verandas afford spacious and convenient promenades, and during the cold weather over 15,000 square feet of them are encased in glass, enabling the most delicate invalid to enjoy the sunshine and fine waterview . . . A spacious pavilion with a floor of 7,000 square feet is set apart for dancing, and choice music is furnished by the United States Artillery School Band throughout the year." Phoebus installed Turkish, Russian, thermo-electric, magnetic, mercurial, sulphuric, and hot sea baths to enhance the Hygeia's reputation as a health resort.

The Hygeia, complete with all the modern comforts such as hydraulic elevators and gas lights, was a commercial success. The hotel welcomed prominent guests from around the world, including King David Kalakaua of Hawaii. This success prompted the construction of a second hotel on Old Point Comfort next to the Hygeia, known as the Chamberlin Hotel. The Hygeia Hotel, however, began to fade following the death of Harrison Phoebus. The hotel was eventually acquired by the Chamberlin and razed in 1902.

This 1887 engraving by R.F. Zogbaum entitled "Mars and Venus at Fortress Monroe" captures Old Point Comfort's allure as a resort. Few other locations in the United States combined a waterfront atmosphere with military bands, parades, and young courtship. An 1888 *Harper's Weekly* article reflected the following: "Day after day, in their dainty dresses, swarms of charming girls invade the fort, supervise the 'mechanical maneuvers,' criticize the battery drills, demoralize the 'star gaugers' . . . and only appearing conquered by circumstances when they suddenly find themselves in attendance at target practice and compelled to stand the roar and concussion of the big black boomers. Even around the hotel the military air pervades. The Artillery Band comes in every day and plays in the salon adjoining the great dining room, and officers off duty dine with their friends, and point out the historic spots in the neighborhood . . . and when sunset nears and the bugles blare the signal for parade, hundreds of gayly dressed visitors stream across the moat and through the resounding postern and out over the green carpet of the parade, where they make a picturesque group under the grove of oak-trees; and then the band strikes up, and the troops march out and form a line of battle, and there is a brief quarter-hour of music and martial pomp, and then the officers march up to the front, briefly salute their commander, and are swallowed up in a throng of civilians; and then twilight comes, and an adjournment to the hotel, and an evening devoted to more music and dancing, and the artillery uniforms are evidently as much at home in the salon as on the ramparts."

Little changed on Fort Monroe during the decades following the Civil War as typified by this scene of two ladies in Trophy Park. The fort returned to its pre-war peacetime role of garrison life, and duty became somewhat monotonous. Besides Old Point Comfort becoming one of the major resort areas in America, the fort languished as the U.S. Army reduced its manpower and training. Other than some minor building improvements, no concerted effort was made to update the fort's ordnance. Archaic Civil War–era muzzle-loading artillery languished along the fort's parapets despite recommendations to modernize.

Nevertheless, Fort Monroe continued to serve as an important military installation. Jefferson Davis's imprisonment may have kept the nation's attention on the fort, but it was Fort Monroe's service as headquarters of the Freedmen's Bureau's Ninth District of Virginia during Reconstruction that helped foster the transition of the Peninsula's African-American population from slavery to freedom. There were over 40,000 ex-slaves on the Peninsula following the war, and the Freedmen's Bureau sought to assist these African Americans into becoming a "free and economically independent people" through the development of schools. The leadership of Brigadier General Samuel Chapman Armstrong as commissioner of the Freedmen's Bureau left a lasting impact on the Peninsula's educational community. Armstrong's dedication to education prompted him to establish the Hampton Normal and Agricultural School in 1868. Hampton University, as the school is now known, is perhaps one of the most lasting legacies of the Freedmen's Bureau on the Virginia Peninsula.

A non-military use for the Hampton Roads fortifications was identified during the post-war era. Johns Hopkins University selected Fort Wool as the site for an experimental laboratory studying marine zoology of the lower Chesapeake Bay. The Rip-Raps' frame buildings were adapted for research on invertebrate embryology in June 1878. Once the summer was over, the university ended the project and Fort Wool lapsed back into obscurity.

Fort Monroe returned to its familiar role as home to the Artillery School following Reconstruction. The distinguished leadership and scholarship of officers like Emory Upton helped to prepare Fort Monroe and the U.S. Army for the challenges of the next century.

Eleven

FREEDOM'S FORTRESS

One of four forts located within the seceding Southern states to be held by the Union when the Civil War began, Fort Monroe contributed more than any other pre-war coastal defense fortification to Union victory. Fort Monroe was the Federal bastion that guarded one of the most strategic waterways in the United States. Consequently, the fort provided the Union with a valuable base for operations against the Confederacy.

Fort Monroe's location, design, and armaments all contributed to the Union's ability to retain the fort and to utilize it as a springboard for attack against the Confederacy. The millions of dollars spent on the fort's construction reaped vast dividends for the Union throughout the war. The fort's formidable design made it virtually impossible for the Confederates to attack it during the early stages of the war. Fort Monroe could eventually boast of mounting the most extensive and advanced array of artillery found in any fixed, permanent fortification in the

United States. Armaments, like the Rodman guns pictured here, provided Fort Monroe with a powerful defensive capability which the Confederates could never counter. Furthermore, the fort's location on Old Point Comfort enabled the U.S. Navy to resupply Fort Monroe at will. This position at the entrance to Hampton Roads effectively blockaded the Confederate ports of Norfolk, Portsmouth, and Richmond and would contribute greatly to the capture of these important industrial centers.

Fort Monroe's strengths enabled it to serve as a valuable base for operations against the Confederacy. Beginning with the Civil War's first amphibious operation to capture Hatteras Inlet in August 1861, numerous campaigns were launched from the fort. Fort Monroe played a critical role in preparing Terry's Expedition to Fort Fisher, North Carolina, in January 1865, which was the war's last amphibious campaign. Furthermore, the conflict's largest amphibious operation, McClellan's Peninsula Campaign, was initially based at Fort Monroe.

As Commander-in-Chief, President Abraham Lincoln gained campaign experience when he traveled to Fort Monroe in early May 1862 and coordinated the capture of Norfolk. All of these operations proved Fort Monroe worthy of its pre-war title of "the Key to the South." The Lincoln Gun, pictured on the parade field in the 1880s as it still remains today, is a reminder of the fort's major role during the Civil War.

Tens of thousands of soldiers passed through Fort Monroe en route to service elsewhere throughout the South. The fort and its outlying camps became a beehive of activity supporting various campaigns. The Engineer's Wharf and the Baltimore Wharf (pictured here) welcomed all of these soldiers and many of the war's most important Union leaders. President Abraham Lincoln, Secretary of War Edwin Stanton, Ulysses Simpson Grant, George McClellan, and Ben Butler all utilized the fort as a strategic headquarters for planning and executing several significant operations.

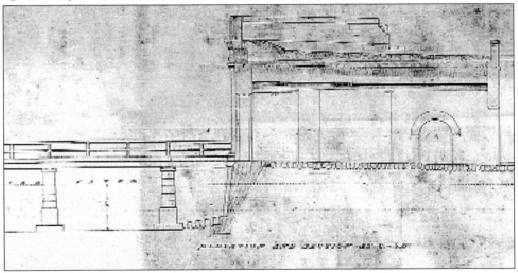

Perhaps Fort Monroe's most enduring contribution to the Union war effort is the "contraband of war" decision. Ben Butler brought the Civil War a step closer to becoming a war about freedom when he issued his May 24, 1861 contraband declaration. Butler used his knowledge of the law and his military right to redefine the war's purpose. The contraband legacy would forever change America. Fort Monroe well deserved the title of "Freedom's Fortress" when it became a magnet for slaves seeking freedom. Butler's decision weakened the Confederate economy and war effort, while the ex-bondsmen supported Union military operations.

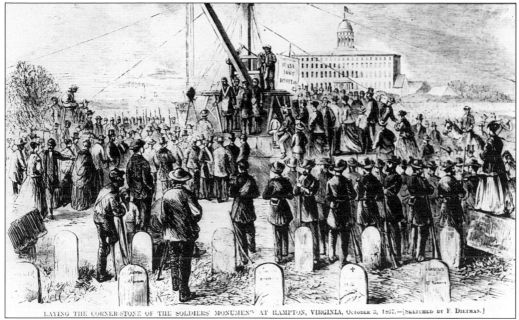

LAYING THE CORNER-STONE OF THE SOLDIERS' MONUMENT AT HAMPTON, VIRGINIA, OCTOBER 3, 1867.—[SKETCHED BY F. DIELMAN.]

Ben Butler's legacy on the Peninsula extended beyond his military leadership and abolitionist activities. When three homes for disabled veterans were established in the North shortly after the war's conclusion, Butler petitioned Congress to establish a similar facility near Fort Monroe. The Chesapeake Female College, which had served as a hospital for Union troops stationed at Fort Monroe, was selected as the site for the National Home for Disabled Volunteer Soldiers and Seamen. Even before this decision was made, a national cemetery was established near the college. A solemn ceremony was held on October 3, 1867, dedicating the soldier's monument honoring the Federal soldiers who had died striving to preserve the Union.

Fort Monroe's Civil War service was outstanding. No other seacoast fortification in the United States served the nation in such a conspicuous fashion from the war's beginning to the conflict's conclusion. Fort Monroe was a key component in the Union victory, having served as a base for launching amphibious operations against Confederate ports and providing sanctuary for slaves seeking freedom. Fort Monroe is one of the few Civil War–era forts still serving as an active military installation. Yet the fort's Civil War legacy is still evident virtually everywhere you walk along its parapets. Fort Monroe's dynamic role as "Freedom's Fortress" will stand forever as a symbol of our nation's dedication to liberty.

PHOTO CREDITS

The Casemate Museum provided the images for this publication except for the following images, noted by page number with an "a" for the first image and a "b" for the second: Jack Boyenton 82a; City of Hampton 70a; Library of Congress 66a, 84a; Library of Virginia 6a; Michael McAfee 2; Mariners' Museum 26; Museum of the Confederacy 84b; National Archives 50b; David Neff 96a; John Moran Quarstein 12b, 49b, 62b; U.S. Army Historical Institute 65, 90b, 92b, 109; U.S. Naval Historical Center 68b; Virginia War Museum 28b, 39 inset, 41b, 44b, 63, 66b, 90a.

ACKNOWLEDGMENTS

I will always remember my first visit to Fort Monroe. It was 1960 and I was seven years old. The fort fascinated me and I found every aspect of its history enthralling. The combination of cannons, casemates, and Civil War history was just too much for me to ignore. My years spent living on Fort Monroe with my parents, Mary and Vernon Quarstein, left an indelible mark on me and inspired me to write this book. I lived for several years at 165 Bernard Road overlooking the parade ground with the Lincoln Gun pointing directly at my house. I volunteered at the Casemate Museum with my mother, worked as a lifeguard for seven years on Old Point Comfort's beaches, and worshipped at the Chapel of the Centurion. It was a wonderful experience that prompted me to write this book.

I am indebted to so many people for helping me create *Fort Monroe: The Key to the South*. First, I must honor Dr. Chester Bradley, the founder of the Casemate Museum. Dr. Bradley took me under his wing and, along with my mother, Mary, guided me to respect and love the fort's tremendous Civil War heritage. Dennis Mroczkowski, the current director of the Casemate Museum, was a great co-author and is a very good friend. His son, Douglas Mroczkowski, helped Dennis identify the images featured in this volume from the Casemate Museum's comprehensive and extensive collection of maps, paintings, prints, and photographs. My son, John Moran Quarstein, also supported the project with several selections from his collection and his marvelous mother, Martha, helped to prepare the text for publication.

I would be remiss if I did not thank my photo editors: Sarah Goldberger, David J. Johnson, J. Michael Moore, and Tim Smith. Their combined talents helped to make this visual history such an interesting volume. My deepest appreciation must also be extended to J. Michael Moore and Elizabeth A. Hobi for their fine research assistance. Thanks must also be extended to Jack Boyenton, David Neff, and Michael McAfee for the loan of images from their collections for inclusion in this book. Everyone associated with this project did their best to make *Fort Monroe: The Key to the South* such an enjoyable book to produce.

Finally, I must honor all of the soldiers, sailors, politicians, and civilians whose service made Fort Monroe the key to the South. Their efforts defined Fort Monroe as "Freedom's Fortress," and left behind them a tremendous record of leadership and devotion to duty.

Drugs in Sport

Drug use and abuse is perhaps the biggest challenge facing spo   However, in the eye of the storm of public and press opinion and with m   and morals at stake it can be difficult to gain a clear perspective on this complex issue. *Drugs in Sport* is the most comprehensive and accurate text available on the subject. Now in a fully revised and updated fifth edition, taking into account the latest regulations, methods and landmark cases, the book explores the hard science behind drug use in sport, as well as the ethical, social, political and administrative context. Key topics include:

- Mode of action and side effects of each major class of drugs used in sport
- Discussion of cutting-edge issues, including gene doping
- The latest doping control regulations of the World Anti-Doping Agency (WADA)
- Methods and advances in doping control, including new intelligence-led detection policies
- The use of Therapeutic Use Exemption for certain drugs banned in sport
- Issues surrounding non-prohibited substances and ergogenic aids
- An assessment of the prevalence of drug taking in sport

Accessibly written, extensively referenced, and supported throughout with illustrative case studies and data, *Drugs in Sport* provides a comprehensive, objective resource for students and researchers, athletes, sports scientists, coaches, journalists, sports administrators and policymakers.

David R. Mottram is Emeritus Professor of Pharmacy Practice at Liverpool John Moores University. His research interests have centred on the use of drugs in sport with particular emphasis on over-the-counter drugs. He is the editor of 4 previous editions of Drugs in Sport.